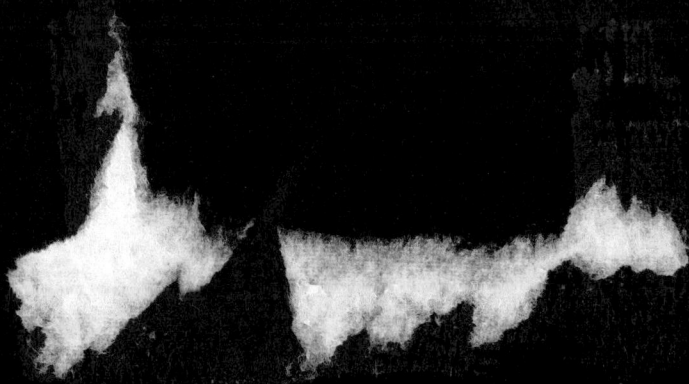

SPEAK OUT!

Günter Grass

SPEAK OUT!
SPEECHES, OPEN LETTERS, COMMENTARIES

Translated by Ralph Manheim

Introduction by Michael Harrington

London

Secker & Warburg

First published in England 1969 by
Martin Secker & Warburg Limited
14 Carlisle Street, Soho Square, London, W1V 6NN

SBN: 436 18787 6

Printed in the United States of America

EDITORIAL NOTE

With the approval of the author, certain cuts have been made in some of the following texts. Passages referring to incidents and people of strictly local and limited topical interest have been deleted. The sequence is chronological, covering the period from summer 1965, when Günter Grass gave a series of election speeches, to September 1968. Up to p. 116 the texts in this volume are a selection from *Über das Selbstverständliche*, published in 1968 by Hermann Luchterhand Verlag. Date and place of publication of the later texts are given in headnotes.

INTRODUCTION

By Michael Harrington

Günter Grass is best known to American and English readers as the most serious comic genius of the postwar period, a Rabelaisian surrealist who has incarnated the Hitler years and their frantic aftermath in profound fantasies. That, one might say, is accomplishment enough for it places him in the very front rank of the contemporary imagination. Yet, as this collection makes clear, Grass is more than a brilliant, and quite probably great, writer. He also represents the very best of the German democratic tradition. It can be said without exaggeration that Günter Grass and men like him are the only hope that Germany will finally transcend the terrible, and still unresolved, heritage of Nazism.

Moreover, if the politics of these essays are important for an understanding of the almost quarter of a century since the fall of the Third Reich, they are particularly relevant to the present and immediate future. For German democracy is now challenged by militant, youthful critics on the confrontation Left who insist that parliaments and elections are a hoax, and by a resurgent Right with strong ties to the Nazi past in the National Democratic Party. And, at the very same time, Walter Ulbricht's "Democratic Republic" has joined with the Russians in the imperialist suppression of the Czechoslovakian freedom movement and thus helped to reintroduce the mood of Cold War in central Europe. Under these circumstances, Günter Grass's insights take on an imperative urgency.

Grass, as he himself recounts in his "Speech to a Young Voter," was born in Danzig in 1927. At fourteen he was a member of the Hitler Youth, by seventeen he was serving in the Panzers, and at eighteen he was in an American prisoner-of-war camp. It was then that he began to understand the crimes which his generation committed in the name of the future. "When I was nineteen," he writes, "I began to have an inkling of the guilt our people had knowingly and unknowingly accumulated, of the burden of responsibility which my generation and the next would have to bear."

So Günter Grass is not the "good German" who seeks to avoid any responsibility for the Nazi horrors by claiming that he did not know about them. He voluntarily assumes a tragic responsibility for crimes which he did not himself commit but in which he feels himself, and his country, implicated. And it is that clear and moral rejection of the unspeakable horrors of Hitlerism which makes him an opponent of the established powers in both Germanys and, indeed, throughout the world.

For that matter, Grass's summary survey of postwar politics posits a sort of symbiotic relationship between reaction in the capitalist West and Communist East. "For more than twenty years every attempt to free Western democracy from its reactionary strait jacket was defamed as open Communism or crypto-Communism. The anti-Communism enthroned in the West is the greatest triumph Communism could have achieved. It struck keen-sighted democrats blind. . . . This explains why parliamentary democracies have supported a corrupt feudal system in Persia, this is what made it possible for the anachronistic dictators of Spain and Portugal to stand side by side with Konrad Adenauer on the platform of anti-Communism; while today the United States and its sullen satellites support the dictator Ky merely because he calls himself an anti-Communist, just as the Soviet Union and its equally sullen satellites support the dictator Nasser merely because he represents himself as socialist, anti-capitalist, anti-imperialist. . . . A corrupted Communism that has developed into a dictatorship of the bureaucracy is confronted by democracies whose parliaments are subservient to lobbies, whose formally free elections have more and more become a farce."

Günter Grass has applied these uncompromising critical categories to his own country. Americans who thought of Germany as an "economic miracle" in which God, capitalism and anti-Communism triumphed have been shocked and surprised by some of the events of the past several years: riots on the Left and electoral progress by the neo-Nazi Right. As an active participant in his country's democratic Left—the Social Democratic Party (S.P.D.)—Grass, as these essays show, was aware of these disturbing, even explosive, tendencies all along.

He described Axel Cäsar Springer, the West German press lord, as a "co-chancellor, who is accountable to no Parliament, who cannot be voted out of office, and who has set up a state within the state. . . ." In 1965, when Willy Brandt, the S.P.D.'s candidate for Chancellor, was vilified for having participated in the anti-Hitler emigration, Grass said that the resultant defeat meant that the Christian Democrats would lead the dance around the golden calf for another four years. And there is a particular scorn, and even horror, for the Christian Democrats when they make a former commentator on the Nazi race laws, Hans Globke, a high administration official—or install a former Hitler Party member as the Chancellor of an officially anti-Hitler Germany.

All of these charges have, of course, been made by Walter

Ulbricht and the East German Communists—only they do not apply the same standards of morality to themselves. Grass does it for them. The "Free German Youth" (F.D.P.) are likened to the Hitler Youth, the army is characterized as built upon Prussian militarism, and East Germany's ossified Stalinism is invidiously compared with the yearning for freedom in Czechoslovakia.

Indeed, Grass is particularly outraged by the ways in which leaders on both sides of the German iron curtain falsified the heroic general strike and rising of the East German workers in 1953. For Grass, the event was a "worker's rising of clearly social democratic nature." For Ulbricht, it was a fascist putsch, and for the West Germans (with important exceptions like Willy Brandt) it was a "people's movement" without class or political character. Where, Günter Grass asks, is his generation, which was so helpless in the face of this enormous sacrifice?

And yet Grass, for all of his active commitment to Social Democracy and the S.P.D., is not a party-liner of any kind. When Willy Brandt and the other leaders were preparing the Great Coalition with the Christian Democrats, he pleaded with them not to thus legitimate the foreign and domestic policies of Adenauer's Germany. Yet, as he wrote in 1967 when the coalition had become official reality, it was not so much the cause as the consequence of the crisis of German democracy. The real roots were oligarchic domination of the parties, the powerful drive to a political pragmatism which undermined parliamentary control and made special interests all-powerful.

Out of this understanding of the profoundly negative tendencies in his country's recent history, Grass is able to come to terms with the New Left—and the New Right—in Germany today. The fact that the youth regard democracy as a fraud is a result of the structural hypocrisies of the society. And, says Grass, the disillusionment was sped by the Social Democratic attack on the youth from the Right. In his May Day, 1968, speech, he argues that there is no security from false prophets unless there is reform, including the democratization of the parties and the abrogation of the NATO Treaty through a general European peace agreement with the Warsaw Pact states.

And yet in thus underlining what is understandable—and valuable—in the youthful protest, Grass does not lose his faith in democracy. He believes that the S.P.D. can, and should, give democratic expression to the unrest which has brought the students into the street. And throughout these essays that is perhaps the pervasive theme: the commitment to democracy and freedom as it is expressed in an honest confrontation with the realities of German politics.

In one essay (not included in this volume), Grass is seeking to answer the question, "What is the German fatherland?" And his own response is: "Let us be builders of cities! . . . Thus will the question, 'What is the German fatherland?' be realistically answered. We need only reason and something of that pioneer spirit which inspired the German immigrants in America who built their Frankfurt, Hamburg and Berlin in the Middle West. We must not seek after the lost provinces [of the old Germany —M.H.] but rather to regain that essence which once was the German fatherland." That is the authentic voice of the German democratic spirit which, in the tremendous achievements of its labor and socialist movements, once held out a marvelous promise to the entire world.

Indeed, there are some similarities between Grass and a great German novelist of the previous generation, Thomas Mann. Both started out on the Right: Grass in the Hitler Youth, Mann as a pre-World War I conservative (his *Reflections of an Unpolitical,* published during World War I, is an attack on democracy itself). The peace drove Mann to the Left until he eventually joined in a united front with the Social Democrats and, later, the Communists. Similarly, Grass was moved to active participation in the campaigns of the S.P.D. Yet for all Mann's enormous accomplishments, he never really did find a political correlative to his philosophic opinions (I have described his odyssey in *The Accidental Century*). He died filled with fear of the future but uncertain of how to resist the trends which frightened him. Grass has, I think, made a deeper, and certainly a more activist, commitment than Mann. And it goes beyond that periodic flurry of electoral activity which has involved American writers and intellectuals in recent years. It is more substantial and fundamental than that.

For all his criticisms of his own party and society, Günter Grass rightly concludes, "To the question: 'Where do you stand today?' I reply: 'I remain a Social Democrat.'"

CONTENTS

LIST OF ABBREVIATIONS

C.D.U. *Christlich Demokratische Union—Christian Democratic Union*

C.S.U. *Christlich Soziale Union—Christian Social Union, sister party of C.D.U.*

D.D.R. *Deutsche Demokratische Republik—German Democratic Republic*

D.F.U. *Deutsche Friedens-Union—German Peace Union*

F.D.P. *Freie Demokratische Partei—Free Democratic Party*

N.P.D. *Nationaldemokratische Partei Deutschlands—National Democratic Party*

S.D.S. *Sozialistischer Deutscher Studentenbund—Socialist Student League*

S.P.D. *Sozialdemokratische Partei Deutschlands—Social Democratic Party*

Günter Grass entered the political arena in 1965, as active combatant for the S.P.D., the German Social Democratic Party, delivering fifty-two election speeches throughout Germany. Party chief of the S.P.D., and hence candidate for the Chancellorship should his party win, was Willy Brandt, then still Mayor of West Berlin; his opponent in the election, Ludwig Erhard, was then party chief of the C.D.U., the Christian Democratic Union, and the immediate successor of Konrad Adenauer.

Willy Brandt lost to Ludwig Erhard, who was later to be replaced by Kurt Georg Kiesinger, on whom the German Chancellorship was conferred in 1966.

On October 9, 1965, Günter Grass summed up his experience as political speaker in the acceptance speech he gave on receiving the most important literary accolade in West Germany, the Georg Büchner Prize, awarded annually by the Darmstadt Academy of Language and Literature. This address is entitled "On the Self-Evident."

SPEAK OUT!

THE ISSUE

Election speech delivered summer 1965.

Much-solicited voters, you who have made up your minds and you who have not! I wish to address all those who figure anonymously in the "no opinion" columns of the Emnid or Allensbach public opinion polls. I request the attention of those who have just turned twenty-one. Article 38 of our Basic Law[1] entitles them to vote. I address all those who are aware that in our parliamentary democracy the citizen is sovereign.

This campaign tour is a conscious break with tradition. I am not a candidate, nor do I represent any of our powerful lobbies, such as the homeowners or farmers. I shall not even venture to discuss the affairs of my own occupational group. Who, for example, would be interested in hearing about the writer's position on taxation? But as a Berliner who is not permitted to vote,[2] I shall attempt to give you food for thought.

[1] The "Grundgesetz," Germany's constitution.
[2] Because of the special status of Berlin, Berliners cannot participate in the Federal voting.

We are not financed by any political party. That is why we charge admission, hoping that we are worth one mark. After all, we are not selling old shoes or white elephants. The organizers of this tour are the League of Liberal Students, the Social Democratic University League, and myself. If we go broke, we shall have to reach deep into our own pockets. But we believe we have a head for figures and expect to keep out of the red. We even hope to show a profit from our two weeks' trip to Hamburg, Kiel, Münster and Bonn—yes, Bonn!—to Aachen, Moers, Cologne, Würzburg—yes, Catholic Würzburg!—Nuremberg, Freiburg, Tübingen, Heidelberg, Mainz and Munich.

What will be done with the surplus money? The days of the Julius Tower[1] are past. We will invest it. With our newly won capital and with the help of generous German publishing houses we mean to purchase from three to five libraries which will assuredly find their beneficiaries, that is, readers, once we have donated them to from three to five army posts.

It seems to us that "Books for the Army" is not a bad slogan. In any case it strikes me as more sensible than the traditional "Forward over graves!" of Field Marshal Schörner's[2] day. We also hope that "Books for the Army" will prove more attractive than the old saw of the legendary fifties—"No experiments"—and the lame variants in which the word "secure" is worn to the bone.

Our first entry in the credit column is that a few army posts have expressed an interest in our intellectual weapons: (1) the 100th Army Aviation Battalion; (2) the 110th Quartermaster Battalion; (3) the 110th Signal Battalion; (4) the 150th Artillery Battalion; (5) the 72nd Artillery Battalion. And we expect to hand the libraries over even before the elections—that is how

---

[1] The Julius Tower in Berlin was used for a time for the safekeeping of surplus funds accumulated by the government during the postwar period in contravention of budgetary regulations.

[2] Ferdinand Schörner, one of Hitler's most ruthless generals, known as "Bloodhound."

fast we work! Both classics and modern authors will be represented. Shelf upon shelf of history, philosophy and sociology. But there will also be good light reading, including detective stories: we have no desire to force culture down anyone's throat. Marx and Engels will also be made available, because the soldiers of our Bundeswehr, our army, are adult readers. (Moreover, one can counter the wicked Communist infiltration more adroitly if one has browsed in *Das Kapital* and is able to reel off parts of the Communist Manifesto.)

Those are our campaign gifts. We have drawn our inspiration from the Socialist Party[1] and its simple but brilliant idea of returning all campaign funds to the citizens in the form of school libraries. Unlike Herr Erhard, who has no qualms about letting the Press and Information Office of the federal government finance his campaign advertisements in German newspapers and periodicals, the Social Democrats have set the example of a responsible attitude toward the taxpayer's money. With the help of your admission fees we shall attempt to vary this refreshingly unconventional accomplishment and hope that our "Books for the Army" initiative will not seep away in the sands of the Lüneburg Heath, but will be taken up by the Defense Minister of the next government. . . .

So much for our finances. And now to the subject: I have never made an election speech before, and for the last few weeks I have been going about with a feeling that is new to me: stage fright. No one asked us to put on this balancing act, and even now Herbert Wehner[2] is probably blowing sparks from his pipe because something is happening that he did not organize. I have received help from an American colleague: Walt Whitman. He lived from 1819 to 1892, wore a waving Biblical beard, had a voice that carried from coast to coast, from Long Island to California,

---

[1] The S.P.D., Sozialdemokratische Partei Deutschlands.
[2] Vice-President of the S.P.D.

and left behind him a book entitled *Leaves of Grass.* It contains free-flowing songs which touch on every part of the country and every trade, on the individual and the masses, songs which gave the United States of America a poetic constitution that is valid to this day. Walt Whitman, a Lincoln of the language. A man who sang of democracy. He had the courage and the humor to say:

"O such themes—equalities! O divine average!" [1]

Let Walt Whitman be our platform. Standing on that platform, a citizen among citizens, we say: "Democracy, of thee I sing!"

I have devised this motto, with which my friends and I inaugurate an exciting trip, as a variation on the following quotation from Walt Whitman: "For you these from me, O Democracy, to serve you ma femme. For you, for you I am trilling these songs." [2]

I designed the poster for our tour. The cock crowing "ES-PE-DE" [3] senses the coming of dawn and, as can only be guessed, is standing on a dunghill.

My speech is entitled: "The Issue." Therefore not a word about Franz-Josef Strauss.[4] He has his political future behind him and is not at issue.

Is Ludwig Erhard at issue? The Emnid and Allensbach polls, our oracles of public opinion, whisper that he is still popular. Is, then, popularity an issue? If it were, we should have to transform our parliamentary democracy into a chancellor democracy made to Erhard's measure. It is to be hoped that our Basic Law will save us from such a falsification. A popular candidate must make presents. A popular candidate must make campaign gifts. A "popular" candidate attaches more importance to the most insignificant

---

[1] From "Starting from Paumanok," in *Leaves of Grass,* Modern Library, p. 18.
[2] From "For You, O Democracy," *loc. cit.,* p. 96.
[3] Initials of S.P.D.
[4] Chairman of the C.S.U., the sister party of the C.D.U. in Bavaria.

lobby than to the Bundestag[1] to which he is supposed to be responsible. Popularity is expensive. Yet though it has neither program nor plan, it is upheld by the oracular utterances of the public opinion experts. It is at issue.

And Willy Brandt is at issue. He stands for a wide-ranging domestic program and a realistic foreign policy; but, the electoral strategists whisper, he lacks popular appeal. What contempt for the electorate! What arrogance sees a Lieschen Müller, the proverbial bird-brain, in every prospective voter! Is televised cigar smoke to be a substitute for argument? Is the democracy of the air waves to usurp the powers of the Bundestag?

An election is an appeal to reason. Consequently my purpose in making this speech cannot be to fire you with wild enthusiasm over politicians and political parties. Our history makes us painfully aware of that. I shall be satisfied if I can merely succeed in giving each one of you food for thought.

This speech was conceived in Maryland, U.S.A., on the Atlantic coast. You may ask: Didn't this man have anything better to do amid dunes, billboards and deserted beach hotels than to meditate on conditions in West Germany? Why didn't he stick to his last and spend his time thinking up the usual stories? Why didn't he write poems about leaping dolphins and the eternally drunken horizon?—Forgive me: desperately as the empty beer cans on the beach tempted me to dream up daring metaphors, I was unable to forget our rich, poor, smiling and morose, easygoing and hectic country, our country that is so battered and torn and yet, all things considered, so young.

The ocean might have been helpful. It invited me to look at things from a distance. The belfries of Germany and Germany's belfry politics were hidden from sight. And only the dull-witted, self-documenting surf, marching toward the beach with measured tread, offered a mild parody of Ludwig Erhard's breathtaking

---

[1] The lower house of Parliament.

ideas about a "symmetrically constructed" society. In short: Bonn was far away. The newspapers were days late. There were no official denials to bother me. And in Maryland no one was aware of the vital importance of quotation marks in the life of the Federal Republic.

But distance makes the humblest of us arrogant, and I was resolved to keep my mind on our German patchwork quilt. And so I turned my back on the ocean, decided to forgo the distance that makes everything look simpler than it is, rummaged through my suitcase and produced the German fare that I had brought with me in prevision of just such an emergency, for example, the Chancellor's inaugural address with its homely motto: "These are times that call for action—in German politics as elsewhere." . . . Bottom-most I found our Basic Law, richly commented on by Andreas Hamann. What splendid reading matter for America!

Article 38, Paragraph 1: "The members of the German Bundestag are elected by universal, direct, free, equal and secret ballot. They are representatives of the people at large, bound by no commitments or instructions and subject only to their own conscience."

Two excellent, powerful sentences. Unfortunately, no reference is made to the crucial question of an electoral system anchored in the Basic Law. For equality of vote implies equal opportunity for candidates. But the Federal Constitutional Court has approved the 5 percent restrictive clause[1] and in so doing called Article 38 into question. Our Basic Law does not provide for discrimination against so-called "splinter parties," because such discrimination is incompatible with the principle of constitutional government.

Article 38, Paragraph 2 runs: "All those who have attained

---

[1] A clause precluding from parliamentary representation any party with less than 5 percent of the vote.

the age of twenty-one are entitled to vote; all those who have attained the age of twenty-five are entitled to hold elective office."

Military service, however—so we read—is incumbent on all males who have attained the age of eighteen. Does this mean that the franchise requires greater maturity than military service? How can we speak of our soldiers as citizens in uniform if they are not allowed to vote?

Recently the army ran a recruiting notice in a West German illustrated magazine. It was headlined with the slogan: "Learn to think." That headline appealed to me. But does it not imply that the thinking Bundeswehr soldier should be entitled to vote?

Our Basic Law is our most valued possession. Never has a German state had so excellent a legal foundation, that is, a constitution providing for so much freedom. Let us carefully and patiently extend this edifice. My suggestions for the next Parliament, which is to be elected in September, are as follows:

1. A definition of our electoral system should be included in the Basic Law.

2. The 5 percent restrictive clause is contrary to the provision for equality of vote laid down in the Basic Law. It should be repealed because it contradicts the principles of constitutional government.

3. Either Article 38, Paragraph 2, or our military service law should be modified. For if a man is subject to military service at the age of eighteen, he should also be eligible to vote. It is meaningless to speak of a citizen in uniform who cannot vote.

So much for my proposals.

I am here to speak of the elections. Who is speaking? A storyteller. A man who is always saying: Once upon a time. Ought he to lower or to raise his voice? America, the Atlantic in his ears—what kind of beginning is that? Oughtn't he to have columns of figures in front of him? Aren't statistics sacred nowadays? And whom is he addressing? His generation. That is, the survivors of his generation. Because the dead are not eligible to vote. Once upon a time there were thirty-eight schoolboys. All of them were born in 1922. Twenty-six became soldiers in 1940, eight in 1941. The remaining four had weak eyes or heart murmurs, so they did not go to war until late in 1944. When the war was over, twelve of the thirty-eight were still alive. Two emigrated. Four live in the German Democratic Republic. Six of the thirty-eight are entitled to vote this fall. So much for my story. Four years of war resulted in a loss of votes. Those of you who are twenty-one today must understand that I miss the votes of those who, more than twenty years ago, were disenfranchised once and for all, some on the road forward, some on the road back. How would they vote today? Is the question permissible? It is a joy to be able to vote. Peace with its electoral conflicts is more exciting than war with its battles of the bulges. A vote is a possession. It is a thing of importance which proves that I am alive. It is more valuable than any campaign gift. Not everything is at stake, but a good deal is. It is not a matter of life and death but only of the four coming years and their consequences. Only? Who has four years to spare? Who wants to be voiceless for four years?

Once upon a time there was a man. He lived in Schneidemühl, in eastern Pomerania. In 1919 he voted for the first time, and voted Communist because he was unemployed. In 1932, after neglecting his right to vote for many years, he voted National Socialist because he was unemployed. After the war he was embittered because he couldn't go back to Schneidemühl, so he voted for the Refugee Party. When that had virtually gone out of existence, he voted for Adenauer and his promise that every citizen of Schneidemühl would soon return to Schneidemühl. It never occurred to this man to vote for the Social Democrats. Why? Did they promise him too little? So much for my election story.

A man comes along, a fellow with a suspicious trade. He tells stories. Does he also have a program? Does he know how to look behind the scenes? Oughtn't he to stick to his stories and leave politics to the politicians, as we leave egg-laying to hens and taxpaying to the taxpayer?—Politics is not an occult science. If it claims to be, it is bad politics. Every traffic sign, every schoolbook is politics. Even a storyteller knows that. True, he doesn't know as much as he should about the labor laws or about rent reform, but he knows aspects of society that are not dreamt of in your statistics. He is able to single out the individual from the mass and give him a name.

Once upon a time there was a midwife. At the school of midwifery in Hanover she had learned that her profession was difficult and responsible, that a midwife always has one foot in jail. For eight years she worked hard for low pay in three different municipal hospitals in medium-sized cities. Her working conditions were such that she often had reason to fear that one of her feet was indeed in jail. Since she was a resolute woman, she often gave vent to her indignation after a ten-hour stretch of duty. She demanded intensive professional counsel and training courses for expectant mothers. Though conservative, the medical director was receptive, but there was a shortage of nurses, beds and money, and the legislation providing for the protection of expectant mothers was deficient. The midwife took an unpaid vacation and attended a three weeks' course at a school of midwifery in southern Germany. She wanted to extend her training. There she saw figures which proved conclusively that the mortality rate among infants and parturient mothers should no longer be passed over in silence. A truck driver at the school of midwifery advised her to join the union. This she did not wish to do, because most midwives and trained nurses are not organized. On one occasion when someone cited the infant mortality rate in a small district hospital, she cried out: "But that's murder!" Although some of the older midwives were horrified, no one contradicted her. Lately she has been telling everybody, even the medical director and the head nurse, that she is fed up. "Up to now I've always faithfully voted for the Old Man,[1] but now I've had enough."

So much for my story.

Herr Ludwig Erhard is up for election. His favorite words are: "upright," "honorable," "merciful" and "of the people." He is quick to take offense. Since he regards himself as the people's Chancellor, any criticism of his person is an attack on the German people. When he runs out of arguments, he asks for confidence and says: "Kindly believe that my intentions toward you are of the best." Toward whom? To which lobbies is he most devoted? To Herr Berg of the Federal Union of German Industry or Herr Rehwinkel of the farm lobby, who is a past master at dealing with Herr Erhard? What has become of his promised "coherent social legislation"? Senseless campaign gifts swallow up sums that we shall miss tomorrow. The disabled veterans are denied what he has thrown to the university and high school students: an allowance. Don't let yourself be bribed. Don't be venal. Refuse it. Don't accept money that ought to go to our war cripples. Be proud. Fight down your respect for Wilhelminian plush and vapid dignity. A man whom no sense of shame deters from using the language of a Joseph Goebbels, who like Ludwig Erhard does not hesitate to speak of "symptoms of degeneracy in modern art," who in other words is prepared to call back to life the lower demons whose retreat we witnessed twenty years ago, who once again, if only out of ignorance, insults our gread dead, Alfred Döblin and Paul Klee, Max Beckmann and Else Lasker-Schüler, in a word all those who carried German culture out into the world, ought not to be up for election. A philistine as Chancellor is an insult to the nation.

Who is speaking to you? A man who lives in Berlin and is not allowed to vote but is determined to have his say at all costs. A man who in Berlin has gradually come to understand in what

[1] The reference is to Konrad Adenauer.

degree and pursuant to what insidious laws Adenauer and Ulbricht, two deadly but mutually dependent enemies, have worked hand in glove for a good ten years. A man who was an eyewitness to June 17, 1953,[1] and has lived to see how that great, sad, rainy day has been falsified in both parts of Germany.

On July 1, 1953, Willy Brandt, then a relatively unknown member of the Parliament, made a strong speech, for the first time warning the German nation against a process that had already begun, the misrepresentation of the workers' uprising. Anyone reading that speech today will note with consternation that all Willy Brandt's statements have preserved their freshness and urgency. At that time he spoke to deaf ears. Is our hearing any better today?

We are called upon to choose: On the one hand a worn-out government coalition of parties which are torn by inner dissension and have demonstrated that they are no longer capable of any serious initiative. On the other hand, the Social Democrats, who offer not only a broad program worked out in every detail but also a convincing personal alternative. But my purpose today is not to go on singing the praises of the S.P.D. and its program. Willy Brandt and Professor Schiller, Fritz Erler and Gustav Heinemann, Professor Schellenberg and Helmut Schmidt are well able to argue their cases.[2] No, I have something very different to say.

This is July. If I speak of June 17th out of season, it is because I should like each one of you who still has doubts about throwing his vote into the balance in September to bear in mind that in Bitterfeld and Magdeburg, in Rostock and Leipzig, in Buna, Leuna and East Berlin there are workers who twelve years ago took a risk for their own sakes and for ours as well. They would be glad to vote. Ulbricht still prevents them from doing so.

---

[1] The reference is to the date of the workers' uprising in East Berlin, put down by Soviet tanks.
[2] Leading Social Democrat politicians.

Therefore I call on the hesitant among you to abandon their attitude of passivity and vote in the place of the machinists of Henningsdorf, the lens grinders of Jena, the construction workers of Stalin-Allee, in order that their uprising may once again take on meaning: They are counting on us. They are still counting on us.

Who has been speaking to you today? A man with transatlantic meditations and with Walt Whitman in his baggage. Who wishes he had Whitman's voice, his breath to sing as he did—smiling and serene, enthusiastic and angry, without fear of listings and repetitions—of democracy: bitter and dearly beloved, forever inadequate, infinitely irritating democracy, yearned for in prisons, complicated and forever contemplating new change; fatiguing and costly, sacred and sober democracy.

Who has been speaking to you? A man who has written a record of Dog Years, who has pumped the stomach of guilt and poked about in ruins and scrap piles for traces of shame. Now he is looking for new material. The cheerful kind. I am sick of having to say: This is what he looks like and not otherwise; he has done this, forgotten that. Now I wish to tell the story of someone who has not yet done anything, who is just beginning, who is young and unmarked, somewhat foolish and blundering, but curious about things to come: Clear to cloudy. Market fluctuating. Silly new fashions. So many schools that it takes ingenuity to stay stupid. Reforms and public welfare. Solid, rather colorless Social Democracy. No more rumbling of guns or oracles of destiny. No more crusades and no more "Forward over graves." Forgotten our moth-eaten, world-conquering philosophies. Forgotten all elite spirit and occidental presumption. That would be a book. Charming, full of laughter. Combative, yes, ready to fight for parks. Uncompromising when it comes to expense accounts. Why not spark off a revolution that would do something about the deterioration of the German hotel breakfast? Then perhaps it will be possible to tell stories about everyday life, directly, without flashbacks and without the background that still discolors the present-day scene: the Thousand-Year Reich.

There are "Democratic Tales" in the air.

All this is something to vote for.

SONG IN PRAISE
OF WILLY

Election speech delivered summer 1965.

Today I wish to provide a reference for a man on whom I am banking, a man who can always count on my criticism, a man who is up for election.

Walt Whitman sang the praises of his President, the murdered Abraham Lincoln: "O powerful western fallen star!" [1]

I shall try, in more sober terms, to sing the praises of a living man: Willy Brandt.

I want him to become Chancellor. What is a Chancellor? Something patriarchal in the style of the Wilhelminian era? An embodiment of the principle of law and order? The usual father figure to whom sons from generation to generation are indebted for their hangdog looks by day and their dreams of vengeance by night? Who is this Chancellor? How does one address him?

[1] From "When Lilacs Last in the Dooryard Bloom'd," in *Leaves of Grass*, Modern Library, p. 260.

Should he be revered? And if so what should be revered in him? Is he a political pin-up? Someone whose picture, hung between potted plants, adorns government offices? An oracle and source of solitary decisions and platitudes that demand public approval? Or is the chancellor merely someone who, on the proposal of the President, is elected by the Parliament and can be dismissed by a constructive vote of no confidence?

The best thing about our state—and on that let us build—is our Basic Law. Here! I carry it around with me in my little bag. A habit that should be recommended to Herr Höcherl, still our Minister of the Interior. Our Basic Law, Article 65, first sentence, says: "The Chancellor lays down the guidelines of policy and bears responsibility for them." This sentence is very clear. But it is often quoted incompletely, or arbitrarily modified. "Responsibility," which here means parliamentary responsibility, is often dropped. And many are those who turn the article into a monstrosity by whittling everything away but the power to "lay down guidelines." No doubt Herr Erhard wished to create one more familiar quotation when, stamping his foot like a very heavy father, he offered the following self-commentary: "I lay down the guidelines of policy without ifs and buts."

His predecessor, Konrad Adenauer, was made of different stuff. He seldom or never mentioned Article 65. But from its elements, increasingly divesting the Cabinet and the Parliament of their powers, he built himself the autocratic podium euphemistically known as "chancellor democracy." When after a rather embarrassing flirtation with the Presidency the Old Man had finally retired, numerous voices both German and foreign hastened to compose high-flown obituaries, as though to consign him as quickly as possible to history and so prevent his return. "The pilot leaves the ship," the voices croaked. Even Bismarck and Charlemagne were dragged in. . . .

After all this indulgence in historical reflections, it is not to be wondered at that frightened citizens in the Western half of our country should remember the sly old fox with nostalgia, although it is becoming increasingly plain that Herr Adenauer's unpaid bills have put his successor in a worse position than he may have deserved.

After all, Herr Erhard achieved nation-wide fame as the autocratic father of the economic miracle. Who can the mother have been?—But now even this miracle has been exposed to the nibbling of doubt. He, the legendary vote-getter, yesterday the incarnation of optimism, has today become the whipping boy of the exhausted government coalition. He no longer cuts a good figure, he inspires pity, which is unbecoming in a Chancellor. The experiment so willingly and cheerfully inaugurated with the slogan "Give Fatty a try!" has failed. Who can possibly provide the quantities of expensive crockery that this touchy and easily offended man must smash in order to prove to himself and to us that Providence elected him to be the "people's Chancellor"? Which brings us to a definition of Article 65 that was not dreamt of in our excellent Basic Law.

What is a "people's Chancellor"? Our constitution knows of no such thing. The public opinion polls, to be sure, give us an inkling of what a people's Chancellor aspires to be: popular! And Herr Erhard is indeed popular. Even Konrad Adenauer is powerless to make good his promise—in which it resembles so many of the promises he has bequeathed us—to "reduce Herr Erhard to his original nullity." Ludwig Erhard will always be popular. But are we under any obligation to burden this justly so popular man a second time with a responsibility which demands decisions of the temporizer and action of the eternal procrastinator?

I ask again: What is a Chancellor? After twelve years of chancellor democracy and the costly interregnum of the popular people's Chancellor, this question has become urgent.

In my opinion, a Chancellor should be a man who is prepared to observe the first sentence of Article 65 in its entirety: "The

Chancellor lays down the guidelines of policy and bears responsibility for them."

So we are looking for a man who will not wipe the ifs and buts off the table and so deprive his Cabinet of all power. A man who does not feel obligated to the "community of the people" and such hazy absurdities; in other words, a man who answers to the Parliament and not a man who unconstitutionally circumvents the Parliament and makes it the milch cow of extraparliamentary interests. The people do not elect Herr Rehwinkel of the farm lobby or Herr Berg of the Federal League of German Industry, they elect the members of the Parliament. Further, I should like to see a Chancellor who is prepared to combat the increasing tendency to pervert our so well-constituted parliamentary democracy and turn it into a television democracy.

The man who is momentarily effective on TV is not necessarily the best Chancellor; I prefer to hope for a man who does not fear unpopular beginnings and who approaches his goal step by step, with painstaking attention to detail. In Berlin a man has demonstrated that our political program is practicable—often enough in spite of resistance both outside and in. I am speaking of our Mayor, Willy Brandt.

He is not a father figure. He makes no claim to be a man of destiny. He is not a brilliant speaker like Fritz Erler. Or a dynamo like Herbert Wehner. I am quite willing to admit that I find it hard to praise my Mayor to the skies. But why should I praise him to the skies, why should I work myself into a state of dithyrambic enthusiasm or try to provoke one in others? Never, as our history has taught us to our sorrow, has a politician justified dithyrambic enthusiasm. I trust Willy Brandt with skepticism. My sympathy takes the form of criticism. I call on you to vote not for a genius but for a statesman who for years has ably defended the cause of Berlin and hence of all Germany in London and Stockholm, in Washington and Paris. Even our large-circulation dailies can no longer make a secret of the fact that the name of Willy Brandt evokes respect all over the world. He does not carry illusions about in his suitcase, but knows how to expound his program. We would be ill-advised to think of him as the proverbial prophet who is not a prophet in his own country. Today he is the only statesman who possesses knowledge, talent and stature enough to implement a foreign policy capable of restoring its actuality to the notion of reunification.

When Willy Brandt says, as he often does, "My political friends and I," it is no mere flourish, but a deliberate profession of a political style that will put an end to the era of "lonely decisions" and "summonses of fate." With him another generation is preparing to go to work: there is plenty to be done. The talk of impending emergency that has been going around in the last few weeks has been whipped up artificially. Nevertheless I say that the emergency is already present! It is present in places where the coalition government does not want to see it: in the schools and universities, in the hospitals and on our highways.—Willy Brandt and his team will have their hands full when they find themselves in the position of a responsible government face to face with the shortage of teachers, the traffic crisis, our sick health policy and an economy thrown off balance by campaign gifts. Labors of Hercules! Willy Brandt and his friends are not to be envied, but there is no help for it: This time we've got to put them in. The stable demands to be cleaned.

We are proposing a new Chancellor. Has he stolen, lied, committed murder? We have grown up with these questions. Every day we read about murderers who for years have been meting out justice, holding government office or teaching our young people. This is the place to break a lance: Not too long ago Willy Brandt was systematically slandered here in our country and, I am ashamed to say, with a certain success. . . .

I am deeply moved by Willy Brandt's long journey from

Lübeck via the stations of the emigration to Berlin, because it reflects a part of German history that I am proud of, though I took no part in it. I can think of other political figures in whom I take no pride at all. Who can measure the harm that Herren Krüger and Oberländer, or a certain Globke,[1] have done our country and our young democracy? Willy Brandt has the moral authority it takes to put an end to this chapter in our history. With him we shall see responsibility in the hands of a man who is not immune to error, but who did not succumb to temptation, who did not go to pieces morally at a time when going to pieces had become a point of honor.

Let me revive the past. The occasion warrants it. When Willy Brandt was born in Lübeck on December 18, 1913, his name was Herbert Frahm. As an illegitimate child, he bore the name of his mother, a clerk in a grocery store. He was brought up by her and by his grandfather, a farm worker and Social Democrat. At the age of fourteen he joined the Red Falcons,[2] and a year later the Young People's Socialist League. At high school, the Johanneum in Lübeck, the son of a working-class family was an exception.

Here is how I picture him at the age of fifteen: a boy who had shot up too fast, robust, rather moody. His political life began in recreation periods. On one side: he alone with his precocious arguments. On the other: the sons of the bourgeoisie, still hesitant but already on their way to the Hitler Youth. The Trave River smells of summer. Lübeck's brick Gothic is carrying on a subtly ironic dialogue with Thomas Mann. But the S.A. is not to be halted by irony. It is on the march.

In 1930, at the age of sixteen, Herbert Frahm became a member of the Social Democratic Party of Germany. His German teacher encouraged him to become a journalist. He wrote his first

[1] Former National Socialists with prominent government positions in the Adenauer era.
[2] Socialist youth organization.

articles for the *Volksbote*. Julius Leber, then editor-in-chief of that paper and chairman of the Lübeck branch of the Social Democratic party, discovered him and became his mentor.

To anyone who looks into the political development of Willy Brandt the statesman and candidate it will be evident that from the early years in Lübeck down to the recent past in Berlin Brandt has never ceased to draw inspiration from Julius Leber and to regard him as the touchstone of his own thoughts and actions.

Let me give you a brief picture of this extraordinary man whose life story plays a significant part in the history of German Social Democracy and hence in the history of our country:

Julius Leber was a Social Democrat who, unlike the politicians of the extreme Right and Left, was a staunch supporter of the Weimar Republic and its form of government. The Nazis and the Communists were bitterly opposed to him. The Left wing of the Socialist Party and the Young Socialists were also opposed to this political pragmatist. In 1931 when the Socialist Workers' Party split off from the Socialist Party, Herbert Frahm, then eighteen, broke with his political foster-father. The years of exile, his practical experience in Norway, where the Socialists were already in charge of the government, brought him back to the ideas of Julius Leber, who was murdered by the Nazis in July 1944. With Leber the resistance against Hitler lost its central figure, its co-ordinator, its head.

I should like to remind my friends and enemies to the left of the S.P.D., who reject Willy Brandt as a mere pragmatist, of this object lesson from recent German history. But I also maintain that when Herbert Wehner tries, in the best drill-sergeant manner, to teach the young outsiders party discipline, he would do well to consider Willy Brandt's development away from Julius Leber and back again. It is not the worst of our twenty-year-olds but often the most gifted among them who feel repelled by our unwieldy mass parties with their bureaucratic thinking and readiness to compromise. Anyone who writes them off as muddle-heads should not be surprised if they abstain from voting or if just for spite—if only to demonstrate their helplessness—they vote for the D.F.U.[1]

Perhaps we cannot expect Herbert Wehner to change his spots and find a word of conciliation. It is easier for me to cry out in considerable alarm to the Easter marchers[2] and Left deviationists, to all those who, for want of anything better and because witch hunting is in the air, are accused of Communism: Don't allow yourselves to be isolated, to be driven into sects and little groups, in other words, to become politically paralyzed; think of the long detour Willy Brandt was obliged to make before he found his way back to Julius Leber, and express your opposition with less fanaticism and more equanimity. Your real enemies are elsewhere. In both parts of Germany they will gloat if 1.9 percent of the votes cast are again wasted on the D.F.U.

In 1933, two days after the Nazis came to power, Julius Leber was beaten up on the street in Lübeck and taken off to prison. Herbert Frahm, then nineteen, was obliged to disappear, because he wished to help build up the underground Resistance. With justified pride he still bears the name that he then gave himself. Here is a man who really, as the saying goes, made a name for himself.

In 1934 the long period of emigration began for Willy Brandt. If we follow it from station to station, if today we read this bitter chronicle of hopes and disappointments, we cannot fail to see what a vast weight of responsibility was thrust upon this young man who should really—had the times been peaceful—have embarked on a course of university study. Willy Brandt's years of study were years of encounter with the realities of his day. The

[1] Initials of Deutsche Friedens-Union, German Peace Union, a small Leftist party.
[2] Originally begun as a campaign for disarmament, particularly atomic disarmament, the Easter marchers arrange protest marches into various German cities around Eastertime.

Spanish Civil War, which he witnessed as the Barcelona correspondent of a Norwegian newspaper, the German seizure of Norway, which drove him to Sweden, brought him early maturity.

When we compare this odyssey of a young man with the catalogue of slanders with which certain of his political opponents try to dispose of him, we are overcome by shame and anger. We are left with the realization that yesterday's bestiality is still alive, prepared at any moment to unleash the dogs of hatred.

In December 1946 Willy Brandt returned to Germany. He settled in Berlin. First as Councilman, then as President of the City Council, and since the autumn of 1957 as Mayor, he has witnessed everything that has been done to this city: the blockade of 1948, the clubbing down of the German workers' uprising in 1953, and finally the building of the Wall that cut the city in two. In all these crises and others he served, he helped, and often enough he saved the situation.

The forty-year-old Mayor enjoyed the fatherly sympathy of Theodor Heuss, our first President. In a letter from the President congratulating Brandt on his election we find a succinct and accurate characterization of the man who ought, beginning in September, to be our Chancellor. Theodor Heuss wrote: "Your level-headed realism and your fearless energy will prove equal to the job."

Apart from a protracted stay in France, I have lived in Berlin since 1953. Whatever I may like or not like about Berlin, I have been able to express my feelings, to laugh, grumble and curse without stint. And if today, after all our crises and the crushing weight of the Wall, I ask myself why it is still possible to live here, to laugh, grumble and curse, and to work in freedom, my answer is: The people of Berlin, including myself, owe all this first and foremost to Willy Brandt and to those virtues of his to which Theodor Heuss called attention: his level-headedness and his energy.

In the late summer of 1961 Willy Brandt declared: "We have

lived through hard weeks. We were on the brink of war. . . ." Those words were not spoken casually. But while he was doing his job and carrying the responsibility not only for the city of Berlin but also for Hamburg, Münster, Aachen, Cologne, Würzburg, Munich and Bonn—yes, also for Bonn and the whole Federal Republic—Konrad Adenauer held that *his* job was to stab Willy Brandt in the back. On August 14, 1961—the year of the Wall and an election year—he, speaking in Regensburg, made his last attempt to assassinate the character of his political adversary. He did not shrink from bringing up Willy Brandt's illegitimate birth. O ye twentieth-century pharisees and guardians of virtue, legitimate birth is not a title of distinction. Illegitimate birth is not a taint. Such is the view of Christianity. Such is the view of our Basic Law. But you, Herr Adenauer, chose treachery.

The Mayor of Berlin did not allow himself to be deflected from the work he had undertaken. He brought men like Professor Schiller[1] to Berlin. The reconstruction work that has been done here in the last few years should be taken as an example. The energy with which a beleaguered city has been transformed into a thriving metropolis and the political acumen with which Willy Brandt carved from Ulbricht's bludgeon a boomerang that found its way back to the Central Committee—this energy and acumen should be put into the service of the entire Federal Republic.

You are faced with a choice. Over there in Leipzig, Rostock and Magdeburg the eyes of seventeen million fellow Germans are upon us. Their patience has worn thin and their distrust has put on fat. They abominate the irresponsible seventeenth of June celebrations which year after year have falsified the tragic workers' uprising, misrepresenting it more and more as a national revolt; they detest pompous lies and Sunday speeches. Look into the records, read Arnulf Baring's book on the seventeenth of June

---

[1] Leading Social Democrat economist.

and learn to understand this twelve-year-old swindle. The bourgeoisie of all shadings stayed home. It was an uprising of the workers that shook Ulbricht's dictatorship for a few hours. He has been sitting less comfortably ever since.

Willy Brandt was the first man to issue a warning against the falsification of the workers' uprising. For while in the Soviet-occupied zone workers were still being arrested in the factories, the authorities in Bonn were already beginning to spin out the myth of a national revolt. Urgently Brandt called attention to the world-wide echo of the workers' uprising. I quote: "As we have all had occasion to read, these events have done more for the position of Germany in the world, they have done more to promote international confidence in the democratic forces in our nation than all the actions of the Federal Government taken together." This indictment is still valid.

Now perhaps you will ask: Is he trying, now in July, to deliver a belated June 17th oration? What has all this to do with social security and the crisis in education, with the traffic problem and all our common tasks, in other words with the parliamentary elections and their underlying theme: the Chancellorship? Highly as I esteem the broad and well-documented program of the S.P.D., I have not come here today to explain Georg August Zinn's "Master Plan for Hesse." For one thing, I lack the specialized knowledge. My purpose today lies elsewhere. Compatriots in East Germany have asked me to remind you of their existence, to prod the wound that is healing far too quickly. In 1953, after the collapse of the workers' uprising, public life in West Germany continued as if nothing had happened. Parliamentary elections were in the offing. A serious discussion of the German workers' uprising, which, both in its spontaneous, successful beginnings and in its defeat, had an unmistakably Social Democratic character, would not have fitted in with the Christian Democratic conception of an election campaign. The one thing that interested the Christian Democrats was to blacken Social Democracy. Four years ago—the architectural wonder of our day, the Wall across Berlin, was not yet complete—the Christian Democrats took the same attitude. Justification enough, I believe, for speaking today of June 17th and of the expectations of our compatriots who are not privileged to vote. I should like those citizens who have scruples about voting on September 19th to remember how many men and women in Mecklenburg, Saxony and Thuringia would be glad to vote in your place. Don't be in too much of a hurry to throw away the suffrage we have bought so dearly. Vote for those workers in the Zeiss Works of Jena, in the Wolfen dye factory, vote for the twelve thousand workers of Stalin-Allee, who twelve years ago fought for a democratic, socialist Germany, who were let down and have been silent ever since. Vote in order that Willy Brandt, at the head of a responsible government "over here," may defend the cause of our fellow Germans "over there."

ON THE SELF-EVIDENT

Acceptance speech delivered on the occasion of the
award of the Georg Büchner Prize, on October 9, 1965, at
the Darmstadt Academy of Language and Literature.

Ladies and gentlemen:

Why not draw up the balance sheet here and now? I invite you to bite your nails critically, to set yourselves up as a court of accounts. For our purpose is to expose our national bankruptcy, our literary counterfeits, our personified hybris, and the platitude-spewing conscience of a nonexistent nation.

This is the story: Fifty-two times we have blown into full halls to keep the dust from settling. Traversed the map and taken the fatherland to our bosom. Spared our voice at breakfast and soothed it with soft-boiled eggs to make it reach into the last row when the fireworks started. Twisted words into lamp wicks that would throw their light on the young fellow who from the very start had been working his tongue into the heckling position. Learned quickly to sniff out concentrations of the Youth Union[1]:

[1] Organization of the younger members of the C.D.U. and C.S.U.

28

ill-rehearsed choruses whose courage called for darker halls. But the lighting was on the speaker's side. As a rule he had only the microphone to fight. Once he was defeated by his echo. Once his voice seemed to be falling on cotton. Was it in Marl, Hildesheim or Bielefeld? Was it in Scharbeutz that I tried to prove something to somebody without a microphone? Roaring like a bull at four hundred disgruntled vacationers who detested the boardinghouse food, the Baltic Sea and the weather, whose brows were puckered with disgust, who had been running themselves ragged in search of the recreation to which according to the doctor they were entitled. Try talking of "reunification" to a worried lump of fat. Is it possible in a rainy summer to interest a crowd of secretaries and medium-level civil servants, who feel cheated out of the suntan without which life is mere existence, in the sluggish progress of the discussions on interzonal passes?—But Steffen said we had to go to those places: Eutin, Scharbeutz, Haffkrug, Timmendorf. And in the evening, as a reward, Lübeck, large audience, cultivated Hanseatic bourgeoisie; in the company of Siegfried Lenz,[1] that's worth while, the votes pour in.—But suppose it rains?— Doesn't matter, says Steffen. I've spoken to the director of the casino. He wasn't happy: "What, only twenty minutes? In that case you can leave your speech in your suitcase. Make it half an hour and I'll have five hundred people in the casino, the place will be humming. Every one a vote—especially if it's raining. Talk straight to their consciences or they'll pack up and go south. Lay it on: Reunification, need to make sacrifices, interzonal boundary only two steps away, clearly visible in good weather. That's what our vacationers want in this downpour—a good moral hangover. Put a little vinegar in their whipped cream, they need it from time to time, and say 'East Germany' loudly and plainly. That'll shake them up for a good ten minutes. And step right up to the mike. Afterwards we'll serve a little pastry and

[1] German novelist participating in the election campaign.

frozen pudding."—And that's how it worked out. Only in Timmendorf—or was it Scharbeutz?—the sun joined in. And the TV
boys put me into the half-shell of the outdoor bandstand before I
had time to select my beach oration:

"Sea-bathing citizens of the Federal Republic:

". . . For years now you and you and you have pros-
pered with Erhard's C.D.U.—with this assurance the campaign
song of the Christian Democratic Union tries to set our minds at
rest.

"But suppose, just as a test, we try singing this hymn of crassest
egoism to our compatriots in East Germany. Their reactions will
show what they think of us today in Ulbricht's dictatorship:
namely, nothing! Our fellow Germans have nothing but silent
contempt for the people who have been prospering with Erhard's
C.D.U. . . ."

About twenty minutes in this vein without a mike. A few
young fellows let their chewing gum rest for as long as it took to
utter a whole sentence. The barbed passage—"Because people
who boast of their wealth tend to hide their poor relations"—was
hailed by one of the vacationers with "Right! Right!" And as this
beach oration in Timmendorf, Haffkrug or Scharbeutz hurried
toward its end with such words as: "Should the parliamentary
elections on September 19th once again give a majority to the
coalition government under Ludwig Erhard, the reunification of
the two parts of Germany will, consciously or unconsciously, have
been abandoned once and for all!"—When with these words the
actual election results had been painted on the pale-blue to rainy
Baltic sky, the vacationers applauded; they enjoyed the change.

Afterwards a not at all bashful little girl, the daughter of the
local Socialist candidate, presented me with a smoked eel. Which
proves that even on the Baltic coast, not far from the so-called
interzone border, the Social Democrats did not disassociate themselves from my speech.

So that's how it was: anecdotes, anecdotes! Should our only profit from the election campaign be amusing stories that will wear thinner from year to year? Or ten thousand pen scratches from my frantic signing of posters and election speeches? At the end, in Cloppenburg, I was making the deep down-strokes of an oceanographer. And now I would like to know for whom all those eager collectors voted. The whole time I beamed optimism so hard that I grinned in my sleep: Sure thing, we'll make it! In passing I learned campaign tactics. I learned how to return inter-ruptions backhand. Only occasional difficulty with dialects. Cov-ered plenty of ground. Whole days on Seebohm's "Highways and Byways." For whole hours cows to left and right, spotted and im-possible to influence even with the best arguments. But always, with the exception of Erlangen, on time. And on every occasion, while Steffen was chewing away at the last fifteen miles, giving my drafts and speeches a last-minute shake-up: Oughtn't I to cut out the first part in Augsburg and wind up with the nine-point program for reunification? Or maybe the swan song would be better? Typed only yesterday with my Olivetti on my knees, turn-ing the Autobahn into an office just before Ulm. How about try-ing out that aria in seven stanzas in Mannheim? . . . And so with steadily deepening voice I lifted the wobbly Autobahn text out of the baptismal font. From the first to the last stanza: "Peo-ple of the city of Mannheim!" The people of Mannheim were pleased and the cheers rang out. Altogether, applause is a great game as long as it's not replaced by tomatoes. To prolong the applause with hesitation, turning it into a pause in which to have a dialogue with friends living and dead, to wipe it away and re-double it with the next sentence. Out of two thousand faces to pick seven which no amount of arm waving can bring to life, and make them too join in the applause. Anything to get applause. How was it, Gustav? Did the part about the puffed rice go over in the gallery? Maybe I should drop it. Or two sentences with stuffing in between? . . . Repeat the line that gets an effect. Or borrow from Büchner,[1] embroider on *The Hessian Country Postman.* "In 1789 the people of France were tired of being the King's work horse." There must be a way of putting it more succinctly and dragging in Höcherl, Schwarzhaupt, and Lenz.[2] "Small minds bear great responsibilities!" They understood that in Coburg and in Wanne-Eickel, where the babysitters' club was a big success. My invention! At eleven o'clock on a holy Sunday morning. Young couples were able to deposit their kids with the Red Falcons and listen peacefully to my modest contribution. Altogether a successful Sunday. Then on to the New Market in Cologne with Wischnewski[3] and Paul Schallück,[4] addressing five thousand people between two thundershowers. Then hurriedly joined in opening Jan Lebenstein's "monstrous creatures" exhibition. And before I knew it I was sitting with Heinz Kühn and his pipe in a real old-fashioned single-engine plane flying via Solingen and Hagen to Dortmund, where three thousand avid voters . . .

Anecdotes, anecdotes! Is nothing else left? And when in Regensburg I . . . And when on the terrace of the casino in Bad Aibling . . . And in Bocholt it was particularly windy because the Youth Union . . . No!

I made fifty-two election speeches. Small wonder that before and since the defeat first-time voters and undecided voters, heck-

---

[1] Georg Büchner, 1813–1837, German dramatist and revolutionary, who participated in the liberation movement directed against the repressive government of the Grand Duchy of Hesse. Founder of the secret Society for Human Rights, author of the revolutionary pamphlet *Der Hessische Landbote.* Denounced to the police and unable to rescue his imprisoned friend Minnigerode, who was put to torture, he went into exile, first in Strassburg, later in Zurich, where he died. Among his works are *The Death of Danton* and *Woyzeck.*

[2] C. S. U. Höcherl, C. D. U. Schwarzhaupt, and F. D. P. Lenz, all members of the then Cabinet.

[3] Hans-Jürgen Wischnewski, leading Social Democrat.

[4] German novelist.

lers and questioners have haunted my sleep with their manly echo-saturated voices, demanding answers of the sleeper: "Do you believe . . . Did you know that . . . It is alleged that the Socialist candidate for the Chancellorship . . . gun in hand as a Norwegian officer . . ."[1] No! In the morning the election speaker doesn't know the name of the town where he spent the night and where, in the course of exhausting slumbers, he delivered seven speeches and faced up to inquisitorial discussions with people who had only one question in their heads: "Is it permissible for an émigré to become Chancellor of Germany?"

Of course we spoke for weeks on end about pensions, the accumulation of capital, public health laws, and almost *ad nauseam* about security; but in actual fact, and quite apart from the nightmares of a free-lance campaigner, the election campaign of 1965 revolved around the answer to that one question which kept recurring like a leitmotiv: "Is it permissible for an émigré to become Chancellor of Germany?" And on September 19th the majority of the population of the Federal Republic, along with its unconscious "no" to reunification and the sacrifices it entailed, answered the question with a conscious "no." And this decision against Willy Brandt—against Willy Brandt the émigré and hence against the entire German emigration—was a "yes" to opportunism and unreflecting materialism, a "yes" to Ludwig Erhard. It meant that under the patronage of parties that call themselves Christian the dance around the Golden Calf can go on for another four years.

The organizers of this dubious victory made use of every weapon, including slander. Their strategy was to simplify the contrast between two political opponents so persistently as to impose a black image and a white image on the voter's retina and so make it easy for him to choose. Once again the word "emigrant," pronounced in German, demonstrated its value as a word of vili-

[1] Willy Brandt was in Norway during the war.

fication. The humiliation that was inflicted after the war on Thomas Mann, the returning émigré, the slander which even today, long after his death, is cast upon this great German by the culture custodians of Bonn who still refuse to accept him as a German, have been inflicted in still more terrifying degree upon Willy Brandt, the Mayor of Berlin; for in Germany there is an unwritten law which says: Émigrés have no business returning home. Let them, like Heinrich Heine or Georg Büchner, get themselves buried in Paris or Zurich. On the other hand, it was considered perfectly natural that for more than ten years the population of the Federal Republic, including the rising postwar generation, should put up with Hans Globke, commentator on the Nuremberg racial laws, as State Secretary. The parties that call themselves Christian gave a free hand to Konrad Adenauer's alleged political genius: the crime of Auschwitz has been perpetuated down to our own day, rank and office have been conferred upon it. Only in this light is it possible to understand how the imperishable and continually sprouting family of fellow travelers and of active and passive accomplices can have summoned up such hatred when an émigré declared his willingness to run for the office of Chancellor.

We know that slander spreads like a plague. Who was it who today, twenty years after the last epidemic, undertook to find a source of infection virulent enough to poison our whole people, including even our schoolchildren? In their usual hard-boiled manner Herr Kapfinger[1] and Herr Strauss, Herr Adenauer and Herr Erhard will mutually acquit each other of this crime against our democracy; but what true Christian can have had the gall, on September 19th, to give the slanderers his vote in the name of the Crucified One?

True, the Social Democrats too have registered successes that

---

[1] Hans Kapfinger, newspaper publisher close to the Christian Social Union.

should incline us to indulgence; but I refuse to forget, or to gloss over, the facts. A man who has visited fifty-two German cities and tried, often in vain, in Bocholt and Regensburg, in Mühldorf am Inn and in Cloppenburg, to cut the root from under the steadily sprouting hatred, a man who has witnessed the eagerness of milk-faced schoolboys to hound a German statesman who as a boy of nineteen saw through the disguises assumed by the enemies of Germany and took the consequences, a man who, in other words, discerned the onset of a new national tragedy (about which there is nothing new but the date) with all its provincial melodrama, has no right to keep silent.

No! Not another word about Kapfinger, Strauss and their accomplices. But I point an accusing finger at the German public opinion industry and at all those who contribute to it with the spoken or written word. Once again our ostensibly independent press has neglected to speak out, when it has not joined in the chorus of slanderers. And does anyone know of a theologian who has called the slanderers by name in his sermons? What Faustian striving deterred our professors from rising to the defense of the German emigration, represented by the candidate Willy Brandt? What disaster must descend on this country before a scholar will look up from his papers for a few hours and take a position here, now and today?

Ladies and gentlemen:

Fifty-two town halls or market places. I know it is too late to urge you to do the obvious, especially as I am certain you voted for the Social Democratic Party and Willy Brandt on September 19th. I am addressing an audience of the defeated.

Yes, it is no use trying to embellish our defeat. We can pat it and cajole it with sugar: it won't sit up on its hind legs. To anyone who from the disaster of September 19th—and let no one imagine that its only victims are as usual the Social Democrats—to anyone who from this truly all-German calamity is tempted to draw the usual skimmed milk of consolation, purification and catharsis, I say: The goat is dry. Her bleat is mockery and merely recapitulates the election returns. Listen carefully and you'll hear the sorry figures.

I know I'm supposed to be talking about Georg Büchner, but forgive me, the election campaign has left spots on my paper. For five weeks I served as a volunteer, a seasonal worker, and collected votes, the small change of democracy. I walked the tightrope without a safety net—anyone who wished was free to disavow me—I was nevertheless certain of doing something self-evident. It was strenuous. Who finds it easy to avoid every second subjunctive? I flung my voice into full houses and staked on victory. But as my sleeping hours diminished and my hoarseness increased, the indications accumulated. In the train, while the sound of the rails mimicked the speaking choruses of the Youth Union, or at breakfast in my hotel, meager hope debated with doubts that were steadily putting on weight. There sits the silent election campaigner between the *Bild-Zeitung* and the *Frankfurter Allgemeine*. He spoons up the uncouth or well-groomed lies with his soft-boiled eggs. Yesterday's dialect-tinged hecklings ring mercilessly in his ears. The day after tomorrow's anxiety reaches for the first cigarette of the new day. Will this sentence do? Are its arms too short? Is it agile enough to play with an audience? Can I count on the trick that worked the day before yesterday: to play up to the gallery, to think it away, to bring it back into existence and unite it with the orchestra in applause? The unsaid is always left at the bottom of the cup! Dregs! Whatever you do, don't stir them up. Anger might start rutting. It's not house-broken and pisses in all the corners. The stench could turn vast republics of artists and scholars into open sewers.—Speak only half your mind, and pack away your speech about the Emperor's New Clothes[1] between your shirts and socks. What can you do

---

[1] Reference to an election speech not included in this selection.

when you're up against a thousand journalists, amiable in conversation, occasionally gnawed by scruples, but hopelessly sold out? They'll twist your words around. They'll misquote you with veneration. Tomorrow the world will read: "Tin Drummer comes out for abortion." Take a look at your generation. Overfed, with the gravity of beer drinkers, they brood behind the steering wheel, look for parking places, and doggedly negotiate the traffic circles.

Unholy Büchner, come to my rescue. I am supposed to deliver a speech to this commemorative gathering. Free-floating in viscous fame, praised, hated, and amiably encouraged to stand on my head, should I light candles with your name to put us in the right frame of mind and help us to discern the tradition through the overpainting and varnish: Büchner as a Heritage, Obligation and Lasting Commitment? The Hessian Country Postman and the Election Campaign? Büchner, Weidig, Minnigerode and the Consequences? Such phrases bubble from my lips, only too eager to celebrate Easter in the essays of all those boys and girls in the last year of high school who, shortly before the elections, were just delighted to let themselves be bribed, along with Mama and Papa, with a pittance of pocket money for schoolchildren.

No, there is no occasion for elegantly mincing words. This sauce is thickened with flour. Some people may like such pap. As for me, I take sides. I admire and praise the browbeaten and eternally persecuted S.P.D. functionary who struggles with small success against the ignorance that accounts for 70 percent of the Bocholt election district; and I condemn the arrogance of those professors and students who look on politics as mere squabbling between parties, who loathe reality and reserve their enthusiasm for utopia.

I admire and praise the peasant of Münsterland who for the first time in his life, crossing himself before and after, cast his vote for the Sozis. Tired from hoeing beets, he overcame the

Rehwinkel[1] within him, thrice announced his intention to the winds, confessed five times in advance and then did it. In his honor I condemn our high priests of blameless biography, who earn the ludicrous privilege of impersonating the conscience of the nation by writing articles for some semiliberal newspaper. Who has not heard their finely chiseled cries of indignation? Who has not, promptly every Thursday, enjoyed the spectacle of their concerted leaps from the one hand to the other hand? One has a polite *bon mot* for every political issue. Speech fails another, wittily and for several paragraphs. "Deplorable, deplorable," mutters a third in dismay. And so they grind out their daring aphorisms and in their sheltered preserves expatiate, as the demand arises, on freedom of thought, the problem of independence among intellectuals, and the difficulty of writing the truth. Dancing godlike over the exhaust fumes of our society, they diffuse their academic Marxism into the empyrean and turn their attention to the far-off misery of Indochina and Persia, which, thanks to their intellectual elevation, they have no difficulty in understanding. They will turn out an interminable epic hymn to Fidel Castro and his sugar-cane island long before it would ever occur to them to shorten the legs of falsehood in their own country with a simple plea for Willy Brandt. And who indeed would expect this fashionably cosmopolitan elite to rub shoulders with our *petit bourgeois* Social Democrats and their laborious reformist efforts? I myself am convinced that Hessian Premier Georg August Zinn's "Master Plan for Hesse," with its thorough economic grounding, is lineally descended from *The Hessian Country Postman* of Büchner and Weidig, our earliest document of modern political agitation, but what is a Master Plan for Hesse weighed against a utopian view of society in which the pure northern lights and a Marxism trained to sit up on its hind legs meet in cosmopolitan elegance high above the rabble and the

[1] Influential leader of a Rightist farmers' pressure group.

petite bourgeoisie to establish an Elysium without mail order cata-
logues and far from the reek of our streetcars?

No! Do not take this intellectual elite seriously any longer but
by means of laughter hoist them out of the roadway and up onto
marble pedestals in their lifetime. Let's have a closer look at the
conscience of our nation. Its incarnators have rejected all compromise and refused to have anything to do with the common man.
In spite of all temptations, they have never descended to the people but always kept to themselves in perfect purity—praising
peace and condemning the atom bomb, detesting capitalism on
the one hand and the dictatorship of the proletariat on the other.
We were unable to lure a kind word from this elite, except for
the Social Democrats, with their blunted edges and their impetus
reduced to a limp.

Did our knights of the cultural reportage notice that on September 19th they too received their comeuppance?—Because no
one can claim that the Social Democrats, so accustomed to defeat, are alone to bear the brunt of *this* defeat. All those who on
the one hand felt committed to freedom of thought and on the
other hand did not feel justified in taking sides have been voted
down, and are now without representation.

Ladies and gentlemen:

How embarrassing! Here I am frankly cheating you out of the
pleasure of a polite acceptance speech, dragging a profane election campaign out beyond the scheduled closing date and into the
secluded shelter of this academy. Without the proper perspective,
still stunned by the escalating figures on the television screen, I
have entered this hall and given voice to anger.

Rest assured: In preparation I consulted Georg Büchner with
all due respect. He knew what failure is. After his leaflet campaign had failed and the peasants had taken the fine expensive
paper to the nearest police station, after Klemm's betrayal and his
own vain attempt to free the tortured Minnigerode, nothing was
left for him but resignation in Strassburg, slow suicide by over-

work, bitter scorn for the German liberals who even then were the captives of their own presumption and pusillanimity, and the grim hope, born of rage turned to laughter, that the harvest would fail and only the hemp crop thrive. Georg Büchner has given me the go-ahead: Speak out. Be a bad loser. Don't hesitate to shut your eyes to faded merits. If possible, avoid quotations. And do what you have to do right away, before the 19th—votes are at stake. Take careful aim and simply throw your prize into the balance. Now. Later won't do any good. Well, if that's what he said, why should I let myself be intimidated by an academy?

So here comes my lament: If only I had said that in Lübeck or in Augsburg and not only now in Darmstadt, too late! Because if I had given in to Büchner's arguments, I would have captured votes by speaking as follows:

"Citizens of Lübeck, Augsburg, Frankfurt or Bayreuth:

"The election campaign compels me to offend against a venerable old custom. On October 9th the Georg Büchner Prize is to be conferred upon me in Darmstadt. Which means that three weeks after the parliamentary elections the Darmstadt Academy of Language and Literature expects me to make an acceptance speech expressing my reverence for a German author whose unprolific but still explosive work played no small part in deciding me to open my mouth, and influenced the style of my campaign speeches. Consequently it would be an affront to Büchner if, because the date for my address has already been set, I were to let these days of political tension, these days that demand a decision of us all, elapse without taking my manuscript out of my pocket. I beg the officers of the Darmstadt Academy for forgiveness, for today I wish to honor Georg Büchner by invoking his authority for what I have to say about the forthcoming parliamentary elections.

"Should there in addition to Heaven and Hell also be a Mount Parnassus on which the poets of all times forgathered, Georg Büchner would call down to advise me to let him, the revolutionary student of the 1830's, participate in our election campaign.

"After all, the spirit which more than a hundred and thirty years ago drove Georg Büchner out of the country, and pursued him with warrants of arrest, is still very much alive under the aliases Höcherl and Süsterhenn.[1] Büchner's battle cry, 'Peace to the huts, war on the palaces,' has meanwhile flattened out into the evolutionary slogan, 'Prosperity for all'; but both slogans, that of the revolutionary Büchner and the moderate demand of the Social Democrats, can be understood on the basis of the linguistic usage and the pathos of the German Enlightenment.

"Exactly two hundred years ago, in the days of Klopstock, Herder and Lessing, when parallel to the Seven Years' War the Enlightenment came to us from France and Switzerland and struck roots in our Free Cities—and to all appearances it has not to this day been allowed to spread beyond these enclaves—at a time, then, when our country was a piece of patchwork torn apart by big and little separatist wars, Friedrich Karl Moser, the Swabian pietist, complained of the absence of national spirit in the average German, who looked upon the patch of land where he was born and raised as his only true fatherland. Moser wrote: 'Perhaps the average German has never had such a national mentality, such a love of his country as a whole as we find in a Briton, Swiss, Dutchman, Swede, etc., or perhaps such a sentiment has been too long extinct.' Since then not much has happened on the 'national mentality' front, except that today not only 'the mass of average Germans' but our better-educated classes as well content themselves with the patch of land where they were born and raised and make a living. How else are we to account for the steadily deepening division of Germany? Any other nation would have tried to rise above the politico-regional conflicts so as to preserve and extend that which is common to all. But the government of our half-country, upheld by the votes of broad sec-

[1] Prof. Dr. Adolf Süsterhenn, C.D.U. member of Parliament.

tions of the population, has seen fit, though there was no need for it whatsoever, to destroy bridges, to break off contacts which in no way endangered us, and to foster, on the patch of earth remaining to us, a prosperity separatism with the flimsiest of ideological justifications.

"In 1835 Georg Büchner, the resigned revolutionary who had fled from his country, wrote to Karl Gutzkow, the writer: 'Fatten the peasants and the revolution will get apoplexy. A chicken in every pot will be the death of the Gallic cock.'

"Büchner was referring to the failure of revolutionary *élan* in the philistine Germany of his time. But his remark applies equally to our neo-philistine West Germany and the failure of its *élan* to become reconciled with our compatriots in the German Democratic Republic even at the price of sacrifices. Herr Ludwig Erhard is the guarantor of this egotistical self-complacency which has nothing to fear but indigestion. Georg Büchner's chicken in the peasant's pot has grown into an overflowing refrigerator. With heavy step, constantly threatened by heart trouble, we dance around the Golden Calf known as the Economic Miracle, which both our Christian parties have blasphemously made into an altarpiece, while reunification is postponed from year to year. Planned vacations in Italy, the acquisition of a second car, and the coalition government's fear that a successful reunification policy would strengthen the Social Democrats stand stiff-legged and doctrinaire in the path of any attempt to offer our fellow Germans help with no political strings attached. The national mentality of which Friedrich Karl Moser spoke is stifled under Herr Erhard's unseemly campaign gifts. From morning to night we lie about June 17th. Everyone wants reunification if it costs him nothing. Too few want it in earnest, that is, even at the risk of sacrifices. If this were not the case, the population of the Federal Republic would have elected a Social Democratic government after the unsuccessful workers' uprising in the Soviet zone. If this were not so, the building of the Wall in 1961 would have been reflected more drastically in the parliamentary elections. Because no other German party admonished us all to cease regarding 'the patch of land on which we were born and raised' as the measure of all things, no other German party warned us so urgently against accepting 'the chicken in the pot' as a substitute for the solution to our national problem. It was these considerations and not, as Herr Erhard maintains, irresponsibility that led the Social Democrats in 1955 to vote against the Paris Treaty, because they were well aware that the arming of the Federal Republic would bring with it the arming and consolidation of the German Democratic Republic. Today we note with indignation that after twelve years of allegedly strong Federal policy the German Democratic Republic, the counter-state, exists. Lip service to reunification and the preposterous theory that the population of the D.D.R. wants nothing more than to be governed by Ludwig Erhard's C.D.U.—for these are the end result of the years of presumption—have contributed to making our compatriots in Rostock and Weimar, in Leipzig and Magdeburg, turn away from us in bitter disillusionment. Therefore let us all, on September 19th, contribute to opening up a new chapter in the tradition of the German Enlightenment. 'May reason light our way!' "

That, ladies and gentlemen, is what I should have said in Passau on September 7th; I say it today, too late, in Darmstadt. Meanwhile the electorate has spoken. The weights have been placed on the scales. A door has slammed, and it looks as if a few writers, far out on the margin of events, had been careless about their fingertips. Now in their dismay they would like us to join them in the old familiar lament about lost opportunities: If only we had . . . if only we hadn't . . . And are we more to blame than others? We, bent over long sentences in pursuit of the moment; we, with our habit of patiently auscultating the object until it gives an answer; we, with tradition behind us and paper in front of us—we are seized with panic when Power interrupts its nap on the sofa, when the philistinism which only a moment ago lay dormant wakes and puffs itself up into hybris. He who always says "I" has called art "degenerate," he, the Elected One, has invoked that monstrosity, "healthy popular feeling," he who has once again been confirmed in office has given new life to words from Goebbels' thesaurus. Response: lamentations and helpless protests. Sniveling and whining as though the well-known philistine disguised as Chancellor hadn't shown his thousand-year teeth before. Old-maidish indignation in the editorial of the weekly *Die Zeit,* as if the butcher boy had farted in a convent. Why the excitement? That is how the authorities, risking nothing, have always treated writers, in Lessing's day, in Büchner's day, and now again in the day of Heinrich Böll. For, generally speaking, public opinion is more sensitive to an increase in telephone rates than to the dear me's of a few intellectuals who are unwilling to forsake their journalistic idyls. Wouldn't it have been the obvious and civic-spirited thing to rally frankly and openly to the one party that offers a guarantee that the venomous tirades of Goebbels and Streicher will not again be converted into acts? Who can expect a peasant in Westerland to take a sound view of fundamental democratic rights if professors, scientists and writers fail to realize that the inconsequential protests and appeals to decency of men who hover above all partisan strife will never put an end to this evil?

It must be very hard to do the obvious thing. Verily, in this country of ours, the proverbial ship of the desert will sooner pass through a needle's eye than a professor step down from his intellectual heights and pay his respects to reeking reality.

An election has passed over our country. Where were those who only a few years ago still derived a certain radio eloquence from their permanent political commitment? Where, Alfred Andersch, did your eloquent indignation sour the milk of the reactionaries? Where, Heinrich Böll, did your lofty moral outlook put the Christian bigots to shame?

O free and independent writer! What a beautiful fiction!

Whose idea was it that he should wear the heart-warming velvet jacket of the free and independent profession? How many writers I have seen, thus ludicrously attired, walking their freedom and independence like lap dogs! How complacently they manage to hoist themselves by their own pigtails out of the swamp of reality, which always has a tendency to make one unfree and dependent! How dashingly, like Indian wild horses in a color film, they prance: witty, charming, practiced in paradoxes and allegories! For an exalted intellect can transform every unpleasant fact of everyday life into a parable. A writer who does not participate in the catastrophes of reality—for often enough participation means guilt—can construct his own catastrophes and in the last chapter provide the catharsis for them at cost price. Then no questions are left dangling. Every pot has a cover. That is utopia. Utopia, spoiled child of the Enlightenment—unlike her six brothers and sisters, who have always had to work their fingers to the bone for a daily wage—can wish for anything she pleases, and in the end, like Robinson Crusoe, she even finds a friendly Friday.

O ye narrow-chested radicals, who find reform too slow and too complicated. You advocate revolutions that happened long ago and long ago killed themselves, whereas the much-ridiculed reformists, at least those of them who have survived the revolutions of the Left and Right, continue undismayed to make a few improvements here, to carry on the fight for justice there. Adapting their program to the changing times, trembling yet persevering, impeded by compromises, they advance at a snail's pace and call themselves Social Democrats.

I respect them. Their defeat is my defeat, and as for their failings, I look for them in myself. If this speech can provide any consolation, then let it be dedicated to all those old Social Democrats with their skepticism, dry wit and well-concealed sentimentality, who from Flensburg to Garmisch have taught me what freedom costs in Cloppenburg, how far to the left Jesus Christ still stands, and how young an octogenarian Sozi can seem in a crowd of prematurely aged students.

Ladies and gentlemen: I promised to draw up a balance sheet. The occasion has given me an opportunity to honor the German emigration while honoring Georg Büchner. If our younger generation do not learn to look on the emigration as an important, and often the better, part of our cultural history, if, as is again to be feared, our culture and our arts emigrate for the nth time, then it will be time to warn our neighbors, the Czechs, Poles, Dutch and French: Take care, the Germans have again become a threat!—Is this a way to close a balance sheet? How about a few figures that would speak for themselves? In his *Hessian Country Postman* Georg Büchner set out to show the oppressed peasants of the Grand Duchy of Hesse what was done with their tax money—the six million odd guldens which he termed the "blood tithe wrung from the body of the people." But the results of my two campaign trips cannot be appraised in terms of marks and pfennigs. The most we could do was to stress certain points. All in all, we only did what was self-evident. I thank the writers Siegfried Lenz, Paul Schallück, Max von der Grün and the composer Hans Werner Henze who replied: "Yes, of course," when I asked them to participate in our election campaign. To them it was self-evident, and if this speech must have a title, let it be: "On the Self-Evident." To speak up, to come out for reason, to call the slanderers by name. Will the victory of the self-evident be self-evident tomorrow? Victory!—Exclamation point. Victory?—Question mark. Victory:—Colon.

ON WRITERS AS COURT
JESTERS AND ON
NON-EXISTENT COURTS

*Address delivered April 1966 at the Princeton Conference
on the occasion of the meeting of the German literary
Group 47 at Princeton University. Grass's fellow panelists
were Leslie Fiedler and the German literary critic Marcel
Reich-Ranicki.*

They seldom meet, and then as strangers: I am referring to our
overtired politicians and our uncertain writers with their quickly
formulated demands which always cry out for immediate fulfill-
ment. Where is the calendar that would permit the mighty of our
day to hold court, to seek utopian advice, or to cleanse themselves
from the compromises of everyday life by listening to expositions
of preposterous utopias? True, there has been the already legendary Kennedy era; and to this day an overworked Willy Brandt
listens with close attention when writers tot up his past errors or
darkly prophesy future defeats. Both examples are meager; at the
very most they prove that there are no courts and hence no advisers to princes, or court jesters. But let's assume for the fun of it
that there is such a thing as a literary court jester, who would like
to be an adviser at court or in some foreign ministry; and let's
assume at the same time that there is no such thing, that the
literary court jester is only the invention of a serious and slow-

working writer who, merely because he has given his mayor a few bits of advice that were not taken, fears in social gatherings to be mistaken for a court jester. If then we assume both that he exists and that he does not, then he exists as a fiction, hence in reality. But the question is: Is the literary court jester worth talking about?

When I consider the fools of Shakespeare and Velásquez, or let us say the dwarfish power components of the Baroque age—for there is a connection between fools and power, though seldom between writers and power—I wish the literary court jester existed; and as we shall see, I know a number of writers who are well fitted for this political service. Except that they are far too touchy. Just as a "housekeeper" dislikes to be called a "cleaning woman," they object to being called fools. "Fool" is not enough. They just want to be known to the Bureau of Internal Revenue as "writers"; nor do they wish to be ennobled by the title of "poet." This self-chosen middle—or middle-class—position enables them to turn up their noses at the disreputable, asocial element, the fools and poets. Whenever society demands fools and poets—and society knows what it needs and likes—whenever, in Germany for example, a writer of verse or a storyteller is addressed by an old lady or a young man as a "poet," the writer of verse or storyteller—including the present speaker—hastens to make it clear that he wishes to be known as a writer. This modesty, this humility, is underlined by short, embarrassed sentences: "I practice my trade like any shoemaker," or "I work seven hours a day with language, just as other self-respecting citizens lay bricks for seven hours a day." Or differing only in tone of voice and Eastern or Western ideology: "I take my place in socialist society" or "I stand foursquare behind the pluralistic society and pay my taxes as a citizen among citizens."

Probably this well-bred attitude, this gesture of self-belittlement, is in part a reaction to the genius cult of the nineteenth century which in Germany continued to produce its pungent-smelling house plants down to the period of expressionism. Who wants to be a Stefan George running around with fiery-eyed disciples? Who wants to disregard his doctor's advice and live the concentrated life of a Rimbaud, without life insurance? Who does not shy away from the prospect of climbing the steps of Olympus every morning, who does not shun the gymnastics to which Gerhart Hauptmann still subjected himself or the tour de force which even Thomas Mann—if only by way of irony—performed as long as he lived?

Today we have adapted ourselves to modern life. You won't find a Rilke doing handstands in front of the mirror; Narcissus has discovered sociology. There is no genius, and to be a fool is inadmissible because a fool is genius in reverse. So there he sits, the domesticated writer, deathly afraid of Muses and laurel wreaths. His fears are legion. The already mentioned fear of being called a poet. The fear of being misunderstood. The fear of not being taken seriously. The fear of entertaining, that is, of giving enjoyment: the fear, invented in Germany but since then thriving in other countries, of producing something Lucullan. For though a writer is intent to the point of fear and trembling on being a part of society, he still wants very much to mold this society according to his fiction but chronically distrusts fiction as something smacking of the poet and fool; from the *"Nouveau Roman"* to "socialist realism," writers, sustained by choruses of lettered teen-agers, are earnestly striving to offer more than mere fiction. The writer who does not wish to be a poet distrusts his own artifices. And clowns who disavow their circus are not very funny.

Is a horse whiter because we call it white? And is a writer who says he is "committed" a white horse? We are all familiar with the writer who, far removed from the poet and the fool, but not satisfied with the naked designation of his trade, appends an adjective, calling himself and encouraging others to call him a "committed" writer, which always—forgive me—reminds me of titles such as "court pastry cook" or "Catholic bicycle rider." From the start, before even inserting his paper into the typewriter, the committed writer writes, not novels, poems or comedies, but "committed literature." When a body of literature is thus plainly stamped, the obvious implication is that all other literature is "uncommitted." Everything else, which takes in a good deal, is disparaged as art for art's sake. Insincere applause from the Right calls forth insincere applause from the Left, and fear of applause from the wrong camp calls forth anemic hopes of applause from the right camp. Such complex and anguished working conditions engender manifestoes, and the sweat of anguish is replaced by professions of faith. When, for instance, Peter Weiss, who after all did write *The Shadow of the Coachman's Body,* suddenly discovers that he is a "humanist writer," when a writer and poet versed in all the secrets of language fails to recognize that even in Stalin's day this adjective had already become an empty expletive, the farce of the committed humanist writer becomes truly theatrical. It would be better if he were the fool he is.

You will observe that I confine myself, in utter provincialism, to German affairs, to the smog in which I myself am at home. However, I trust that the United States of America has committed and humanist writers and poets as well as those others who are so readily defamed, and possibly also literary fools; because it is here in this country that this topic was proposed to me: Special adviser or court jester.

The "or" means no doubt that a court jester can never be a special adviser and that a special adviser must under no circumstances regard himself as a court jester, but rather perhaps as a committed writer. He is the great sage; to him financial reform is no Chinese puzzle; and it is he, hovering high above the strife of parties and factions, who in every instance pronounces the final word of counsel. After centuries of hostility the fictitious antitheses are reconciled. Mind and power walk hand in hand. Something like this: After many sleepless nights the Chancellor summons the writer Heinrich Böll to his bungalow. At first the committed writer listens in silence to the Chancellor's troubles. Then, when the Chancellor sinks back into his chair, the writer delivers himself of succinct, irresistible counsel. Relieved of his cares, the Chancellor springs from his chair eager to embrace the committed writer; but the writer takes an attitude of aloofness, he does not wish to become a court jester. He admonishes the Chancellor to convert writer's word into Chancellor's deed. The next day an amazed world learns that Chancellor Erhard has resolved to demobilize the army, to recognize the German Democratic Republic and the Oder-Neisse line, and to expropriate all capitalists.

Encouraged by this feat, the humanist author Peter Weiss journeys from Sweden to the recently recognized German Democratic Republic and leaves his card at the office of Walter Ulbricht, Chairman of the Council of State. Like Erhard at a loss for good advice, Ulbricht receives the humanist writer at once. Advice is given, embrace rejected, word converted into deed; and next day an amazed world learns that the Chairman of the Council of State has countermanded the order to fire on those attempting to cross the borders of his state in either direction and transformed the political sections of all prisons and penitentiaries into people's kindergartens. Thus counseled, the Chairman of the Council of State apologizes to Wolf Biermann the poet and ballad singer and asks him to sing away his—Ulbricht's—Stalinist past with bright and mordant rhymes.

Of course court jesters, should there be any, cannot hope to compete with such accomplishments. Have I exaggerated? Of course I have exaggerated. But when I think of the wishes, often stated in an undertone, of committed and humanist writers, I don't think I have exaggerated so very much. And in my weaker moments I find it easy to see myself acting in just such a well-intentioned, or rather, committed and humanist, manner: After losing the parliamentary elections the opposition candidate for the Chancellorship sends, in his perplexity, for the writer here addressing you, who listens, gives advice and does not allow himself to be embraced; and the next day an amazed world learns that the Social Democrats have discarded the Godesberg Program and replaced it with a sharp, sparkling and once again revolutionary manifesto encouraging the workers to discard hats for caps. No, no revolution breaks out, because for all its sharpness this manifesto is so much to the point that neither capital nor Church can resist its arguments. Without a blow the government is handed over to the Social Democrats, etc. The United States of America, I should think, offers similar possibilities. Why, for example, shouldn't President Johnson call on the preceding speaker, Allen Ginsberg, for advice?

These short-winded utopias remain—utopias. Reality speaks a different language. We have no special advisers or court jesters. All I see—and here I am including myself—is bewildered writers and poets who doubt the value of their own trade and avail themselves fully, partially or not at all, of their infinitesimal possibilities of playing a part in the events of our time—not with advice but with action. It is meaningless to generalize about "the writer" and his position in society; writers are highly diversified individuals, shaken in varying degree by ambition, neuroses and marital crises. Court jester or special adviser, both are disembodied little men—five six lines and a circle—such as the members of a discussion panel draw in their notebooks when they get bored. Nevertheless they have given rise to a cult which, especially in Germany, is assuming an almost religious character. Students, young trade-unionists, young Protestants, high school boys and Boy Scouts, dueling and nondueling fraternities—all these and more never weary of organizing discussions revolving around questions like: "Ought a writer to be committed?" or "Is the writer the conscience of the nation?" Even men with critical minds and a genuine love of literature, such as Marcel Reich-Ranicki, who will speak to us in a little while, persist in calling upon writers to deliver protests, declarations and professions of

faith. I don't mean that anyone asks them to take a partisan attitude toward political parties, to come out for or against the Social
Democrats, for example; no, the idea is that speaking as writers,
as a kind of shame-faced elite, they should protest, condemn war,
praise peace and display noble sentiments. Yet anyone who
knows anything about writers is well aware that even if they band
together at congresses they remain eccentric individuals. True, I
know a good many who cling with touching devotion to their
revolutionary heirlooms, who make use of Communism, that
burgundy-colored plush sofa with its well-worn springs, for af-
ternoon reveries. But even these conservative "progressives" are
split into one-man factions, each of which reads Marx in his own
way. Others in turn are briefly mobilized by their daily glance at
the paper and wax indignant at the breakfast table: "Something
ought to be done, something ought to be done!" When helplessness lacks wit it begins to snivel. And yet there is a great deal to
do, more than can be expressed in manifestoes and protests. But
there are also a great many writers, known and unknown, who,
far from presuming to be the "conscience of the nation," occasionally bolt from their desks and busy themselves with the trivia
of democracy. Which implies a readiness to compromise. Something we must get through our heads is this: a poem knows no
compromise, but men live by compromise. The individual who
can stand up under this contradiction and act is a fool and will
change the world.

SPEECH TO A YOUNG VOTER WHO FEELS TEMPTED TO VOTE FOR THE N.P.D.[1]

On the occasion of the Bavarian parliamentary elections,
Munich, November 1966.

Why does this Prussian come around sticking his nose into the Bavarian parliamentary elections? I'll answer that one before it is asked: I am not concerned with the question of whether Munich needs a new and bigger airfield; what concerns me is that if things turn out as there is reason to fear, this election can have consequences extending far beyond the borders of Bavaria; I am referring to the meteoric rise of the National Democratic Party.

Nevertheless my speech is not addressed to Messrs. Thielen and von Thadden.[2] I do not hope to convert Otto Hess, the former SA-Sturmbannführer (major) and now propaganda chief of the N.P.D.—history teaches that if any alternative can appeal to the dyed-in-the-wool Brown, that alternative is Stalinist Red. I am

[1] Nationaldemokratische Partei Deutschlands—National Democratic Party, the neo-Nazi Party.
[2] Friedrich Thielen, first leader of the N.P.D., later ousted and replaced by Adolf von Thadden.

54

concerned with those young voters who are preparing to plunge thoughtlessly into an adventure that can have grave and lasting consequences not only for our country, but also for the young N.P.D. voters themselves.

Because I know my own past and also know the weakness of our German youth for absolute, self-defeating ideas, I refuse to see a neo-Nazi in every young voter who tries to find a home for his aimless indignation in the N.P.D. But I ask these young people to give thought to the fact that their projected decision will be misused by Messrs. von Thadden and Thielen exactly as the idealism of my generation was misused by Messrs. Schirach and Axmann.[1]

Before they cast their votes next Sunday, I ask them to consult reason, that wallflower in our so incompetently governed country. Therefore no generalizations. It is not true that every future or potential N.P.D. voter is a congenital Right-wing extremist. I refuse to regard him as the devil incarnate. Whatever may be the considerations that lead a young man of today to give his vote to this party of the day before yesterday, nothing justifies us in defaming him, especially as there are plenty of arguments with which to combat his decision.

About myself: I was born in Danzig in 1927. At the age of ten I was a member of the Hitler Cubs; when I was fourteen I was enrolled in the Hitler Youth. At fifteen I called myself an Air Force auxiliary. At seventeen I was in the armored infantry. At the age of eighteen I was discharged from an American POW camp: it was only then that I became an adult—or rather that I gradually began to realize what, behind a smoke screen of martial music and irredentist bilge, *they* had done to my youth. It was only then that I began to find out—the full horror was not revealed to me until years later—what unthinkable crimes had been committed in the name of the future of my generation.

[1] Youth leaders in the Third Reich.

When I was nineteen, I began to have an inkling of the guilt our people had knowingly and unknowingly accumulated, of the burden of responsibilty which my generation and the next would have to bear. I began to work, to study and to sharpen my distrust of a *petit bourgeois* society which was once again assuming such an air of innocence. Today, twenty years later, I know that a good deal has been done, that our provisional part-state, the Federal Republic, may have its drawbacks but nevertheless offers democratic, parliamentary guarantees. But I also know how vulnerable this state is. Regardless of whether the extreme left or as at present the extreme right is threatening to undermine its foundations, I hold that it is incumbent on us to safeguard this state of ours— and not by passing dubious laws for the defense of the Republic. No, let us try here and now, in open discussion, or debate if you prefer, to prevent the crime of those days from being repeated.

You may wonder by what right I come here to Bavaria, representing no one but myself, to wage war with democratic weapons against a party which since the elections in Hesse[1] is convinced that its hour has struck? Here is my answer: I will not cite the staggering figures, I will not speak of the millions who were murdered, who starved to death, or who were killed in battle for no reason. I will speak only of thirty boys who were seventeen twenty years ago, who like myself experienced pure unadulterated fear on the first day of our so-called "military commitment," and then, without so much as seeing an enemy, were torn to pieces and destroyed.

Today, with the loud-speakers once more blaring their message of "soldierly loyalty," of "service and sacrifice," it is time to speak of this organized madness. To put it bluntly: the war was not made up of anecdotes about wearers of the Knight's Cross; no, it was a planned and relentless expenditure of young men who sim-

---

[1] In the Hesse parliamentary elections the N.P.D. won 7.9 percent of the vote in 1966. This vote was down to 5.2 percent in 1968.

ply wanted to live and who were deprived of any possibility of protesting against the demagogic misrepresentation of their death as heroism.

Why, then, does a young man of twenty-three vote for the N.P.D.? Is he drunk on the word "radical"? Have things come to such a pass that the radicals of the Left and Right are prepared to swap their resentments? Do the extreme Left and extreme Right regard the Bundestag in Bonn as nothing more than a "hot-air factory"—just as under the Weimar Republic the extreme Left and the extreme Right were agreed in calling the Reichstag a "hot-air factory"? The unconcealed gloating of Ulbricht's house organ, *Neues Deutschland,* over the electoral success of the N.P.D. in Hesse should give us food for thought.

I do not underestimate the N.P.D. Its predecessors, the Reich Party and the German Party,[1] for instance, were heavier-handed. Hatched out under the Third Reich, they were unable to conceal their National Socialist eggshells. The N.P.D. after all has managed to give its National Socialist or German Conservative coat a halfway democratic cut. Demagogic slogans such as "We can vote again" show a gift for propaganda. Goebbels' lesson is bearing late fruit. I remember that when I was sixteen his booby-trap question—"Do you want total war?"—plunged me into a mood of solemn self-sacrifice. . . .

"We can vote again." The implication is that we couldn't before. When could we? The slogan is: "We can vote *again.*"

Why, then, does a twenty-three-year-old vote for the N.P.D.?

The "licensed parties," to stay with the neo-Brown jargon, neglect the question of reunification. All of them? Which party neglects it more, which less? The efforts of Kurt Schumacher,[2] the

---

[1] Small conservative parties.

[2] Social Democratic politician and member of the Parliament in the Weimar Republic; 1933–43 and 1944–45 in concentration camps. From 1946, leader of the Social Democratic Party. Died 1952.

plan of Pfleiderer,[1] Bundestag member of the Free Democratic Party, the first modest steps toward a new reunification policy taken by the Social Democrats under Willy Brandt—all that is ignored by the N.P.D.; what shouldn't exist doesn't exist. Instead of a solidly grounded alternative program, this party offers the old familiar catalogue of immoderate nationalistic demands. When will we learn to distinguish between national consciousness, a self-evident phenomenon grounded in reason, and the substitute for it that is being offered for sale, the hybris of nationalism?

Let me read you a quotation which, more than any nationalistic hysteria, can help us to check up on our national consciousness. On December 15, 1954, the Social Democrats in the Bundestag addressed a question to the government concerning the "priority of negotiations for the reunification of Germany." In the course of his great speech laying down guidelines that are still valid today, Erich Ollenhauer, then chairman of the Social Democratic Party, declared: "The tragedy of the foreign policy of the Federal Republic is that to this day it has been unable to throw off the consequences that followed inevitably from the Chancellor's bid for German rearmament in August 1960, and that in practice the integration of the Federal Republic into the Western bloc has always had priority over reunification."

Rearmament was put through against the carefully pondered "no" of the Social Democrats. And the priority of rearmament over reunification has indeed resulted in a "reunification" policy which to this day has brought no results and for which the C.D.U./C.S.U. coalition has been largely responsible. However, the alternative to this mistaken policy has repeatedly been put forward in Bonn, in the alleged "hot-air factory," by a few Free

[1] Published, in 1952, a manifesto outlining the prerequisites for a reunification of the two Germanys.

Democrats and Social Democrats; today it is beginning to gain a hearing.

And so I ask myself and you:

Is the N.P.D. dangerous?

If it should succeed in frightening us, in intimidating us, then it will be dangerous.

Should the N.P.D. be outlawed?

I am opposed to giving it the advantages of an underground movement. Daylight makes greater demands on a political opponent. Consequently the Communist Party should again be legalized. Only those who are afraid of being infected fear the slogans of the extreme Left and extreme Right.

Does the N.P.D. harm us?

It increases and justifies the distrust of our allies and of our adversaries.

Should we adopt the blanket judgments expressed in the foreign press?

We should look for more accurate arguments. They will be stronger.

Are there old Nazis in the N.P.D.?

Of the eighteen members of this party's executive committee, twelve were active National Socialists.

Is that bad?

Yes. But it is more alarming that a man who was a party member from 1933 to the end, Herr Kiesinger, should today be the candidate of the C.D.U./C.S.U. for the Chancellorship.

Has the N.P.D. a program?

It is for the death penalty and against foreign workers. It raises claims to territories in which, as we are told, the German people has lived for centuries. It is against any aid whatsoever to underdeveloped countries.

Is that a program?

A grab bag of old and new prejudices is hardly a substitute for a program.

Why, then, does a twenty-three-year-old vote for the N.P.D.? If it's adventure he wants, wouldn't a good Western be better?

Will it do a twenty-three-year-old any good to vote for the N.P.D.?

At the age of seventy he will still be trying to hush up and forget a blind spot in his biography. . . .

Can we afford the N.P.D.?

I can only answer that with another question: Did the Sorcerer's Apprentice's broom go back into the corner when it was told to?

Should we kill the N.P.D. with silence?

Let anyone who can live in peace next to a loud-speaker turned on full blast keep silent; I prefer to argue with it.

AN EXCHANGE OF OPEN LETTERS WITH WILLY BRANDT

Published in Die Zeit, *Hamburg, December 1966.*

Dear Willy Brandt:

Before the Great Coalition becomes a reality, before you take your place between Herr Kiesinger and Herr Strauss and are called upon to act as best man at an ill-matched marriage, I beg you, Chairman of the Socialist Party of Germany, the party on which I pinned and still pin my hopes, to consider the incalculable consequences of such a decision.

It is a decision that will force me and many of my friends into a left-hand corner against our will, degrading us to a mere counterpart to the N.P.D. and a politically impotent one to boot. How are we to go on recommending the Socialist Party as an alternative when the profile of a Willy Brandt is reduced to an unrecognizable blur by the proportional [1] uniformity of the Great Coalition?

[1] Offices distributed proportionally to represent the major parties, i.e., not on the basis of merit but of party affiliation.

Your entry into such a government will serve to gloss over twenty years of misguided foreign policy. The incurable conflict between the Christian Democrats and the Christian Social Union will spread to the Socialist Party. Your conception of a different Germany will give way to a paralyzing resignation. For decades to come the great and tragic history of the Socialist Party will lose its direction. The need to adapt itself to the coalition will determine its attitude toward state and society. But the youth of our country will turn away from the state and our form of government: once this wretched marriage is concluded, they will abandon the middle road for the Right and Left.

My critical sympathy for you and the Social Democratic Party of Germany makes it my duty to communicate these thoughts to you. I know that Herbert Wehner is quick to pin the name of neurotic on anyone who disagrees with him. Nevertheless I request you to read this letter to the Party. Let no stone be left unturned.

With friendly greetings,
Yours,
Günter Grass

Dear Günter Grass:

You have formulated fears and misgivings that are shared by many—and by no means the worst—of our citizens.

The Great Coalition involves risks. Emotional considerations and the desire for leadership have suggested a different course to many of us. After serious study of the situation—the hard figures resulting from the parliamentary elections and the tasks facing us at home and abroad—I have been forced to conclude that no other course was open to us.

Now that the Socialist Party has fought its way, not without difficulty, into the Great Coalition, what we feel is something very different from self-satisfaction at having "finally made it." We know that we shall need tenacity and energy and level-headedness if this step undertaken by the Socialist Party is to benefit our people and if your misgivings are not to become a reality.

There will be no covering up of omissions and mistakes, there will be no insipid one-dish political stew. The Great Coalition will be a failure unless it represents a definite break with the policies that led to the government crisis. It is a modest alternative, the only one possible today, to the hitherto prevailing doldrums.

The Socialist Party expects to be judged on the basis of the demands it has always put forward. In a coalition of equal partners government policy will definitely not be directed against the Socialist Party. You have no cause to worry about Willy Brandt's political profile.

Especially at this time, I adjure you, your friends and all our critical young people not to relegate yourselves to the limbo of resignation or mere protest. Such a development would leave the democratic Left of our country not only poorer but also weaker. The conscience of the Social Democratic Party does not operate outside the Party.

No one should condemn us before we have had a chance to prove our present possibilities. For us this is a new start. We shall introduce essential new elements into this new chapter of German postwar history. To this we are pledged; the intellectual community will not be disappointed.

I thank you for your frankness and sympathy, which we should not wish to lose.

> With friendly greetings,
> Yours,
> Willy Brandt

Dear Willy Brandt:

I have spoken my word of warning; you have demonstrated its justification. We outsiders are powerless to halt a development which has been initiated and which I regard as unfortunate. We can draft telegrams and write letters. We can shoot off our mouths; but you still have it in your power to break off this match . . . before it is consummated.

But if it is true that the Great Coalition cannot be prevented, you should at least insist on a Great Coalition corresponding to the political arithmetic of the Parliament. Three parties are to form this coalition. The C.S.U. is the smallest party. It has nominated the candidate for the Chancellorship and put through his election. The C.D.U. is internally torn and consequently diminished in its political effectiveness. The S.P.D. is the largest party. It is internally consolidated and capable of carrying out its alternative program. It therefore has the duty of providing the Chancellor. If the two other parties are really serious, if they really wish to help clear up the mess brought about by the C.D.U. and the C.S.U., they must learn to recognize the parliamentary and political facts, namely, that only a Social Democratic Chancellor is capable of laying down a new policy.

And it should be stated clearly that Franz-Josef Strauss, the former Defense Minister, must never again become a Minister. A man who lies to the Parliament, who attempts during the Cuban crisis to function as Defense Minister in a state of total drunkenness, must never again bear political responsibility in our country.

It may be that the hectic character of the negotiations has blurred your over-all view of the situation. Fatigue makes for hasty decisions. As I write, I am well rested and, despite the tension, calm: Don't overdo it, don't ask people to swallow too much. Such a course might well shatter the Socialist Party and damage our country irreparably.

I thank you for your answer and for the opportunity to answer trust with trust. All of us here wish you strength, courage and serenity, in order that reason may prevail in our country.

With friendly greetings,
Yours,
Günter Grass

OPEN LETTER TO KURT GEORG KIESINGER

Published in Frankfurter Allgemeine Zeitung, *December 1, 1966.*

My dear Herr Kiesinger:

Before you are elected Chancellor tomorrow, I should like, very publicly, to make a last attempt to make you see the light.

I belong to a generation the majority of whose fathers knowingly or unknowingly supported the crimes committed from 1933 to 1945. I know that in many German families the resulting breach has been mended: the fathers' confessions have met with the sons' willingness to understand. You, Herr Kiesinger, joined the National Socialist Party as an adult in 1933 and it took the surrender to dissolve your ties with the Party.

Allow me the following fantasy: If you were my father, I should ask you to explain your disastrous decision of 1933. I should understand your answer because most of my contemporaries' fathers wasted the best years of their lives in consequence of such mistaken decisions. But suppose you, the fictitious father, were to consult me, the fictitious son: "I have been offered the

Chancellorship. I take a passionate interest in politics. It has always been my ambition to play a leading role in the field of foreign affairs. I have had a successful career in my state of Baden-Württemberg. The people like me. Should I accept?" The fictious son's answer would be: "Precisely because you take a passionate interest in politics and because you have ambitions in the field of foreign affairs, you must say no. For you must be aware that this country with its still undigested past, this divided country without a peace treaty, ought not to entrust the Chancellorship to a man who was combating reason and abetting crime at a time when others were dying because they had served reason and resisted the crime. Decency should forbid you to call yourself a Resistance fighter at this late date."

You, Herr Kiesinger, are not my father. I hope you have a son who is opposing your disastrous decision.

I ask you:

How are the young people of our country to find arguments against that party which died two decades ago but is being resurrected today as the N.P.D., if you burden the Chancellorship with the still very considerable weight of your past?

How are we to honor the memory of the tortured, murdered Resistance fighters, of the dead of Auschwitz and Treblinka, if you, the accomplice of those days, have the gall to assume responsibility today?

How is history to be taught in our schools?

Hasn't Herr Globke done harm enough?

Are we to give Ulbricht, the old Stalinist, ground for pointing a finger at us?

Can the coalition of the S.P.D., C.S.U. and C.D.U. not find in its ranks a man sufficiently free from taint to be worthy of the Chancellorship?

I am almost inclined to believe that the S.P.D. has put the

courage of an Otto Wels[1] under house arrest, for it is that party which should properly have asked you these questions. As things stand, it remains for me, speaking for myself and many others, to raise my voice once again, at the last minute, in indignant protest.

The responsibility will be yours to bear, ours the consequences and the shame.

Still respectfully yours,
Günter Grass

---

[1] Leading Social Democrat in the Weimar era, the only party head who, in 1933, protested against Hitler's so-called Enabling Act taking its powers away from the Parliament, with the words: "We German Social Democrats, in this historic hour, pledge ourselves solemnly to the principles of humanity and justice, of freedom and socialism." Wels emigrated to France, where he died in 1939.

THE CONSCIENCE
OF THE S.P.D.

Published in Die Zeit, *Hamburg, December 9, 1966.*

The political forces in our part-state have changed beds. To stay with our image, there has been much squeaking of bedsprings in one quarter and bedroom whisperings in the other. What I regard as a "wretched marriage" has elsewhere been praised as a sensible marriage. Both sides will agree with me that it was not a love match.

We the voters vest our powers for a limited time in the political parties of the government or opposition. Between elections we have the possibility of expressing reactions ranging from admonition to indignation. There have been phone calls and telegrams, the post office has been kept busy. There have been demonstrations; the police have demonstrated their loyalty. I have written three letters and thus far received one answer.

Willy Brandt, formerly Mayor of West Berlin, now Vice-Chancellor and Foreign Minister in the Great Coalition which he helped, without enthusiasm, to bring about, answered by return mail. His letter is moderate and thoughtful; it does not go into detail about my misgivings. I strongly disagree with one sentence in this letter: "The conscience of the Social Democratic Party does not operate outside the Party."

We shall not go into the juridical, ethical or theological aspects of "conscience." We shall not ask: Has the individual a conscience, and if so where is it located? Or even: Can a political party have a conscience, and if so where does it function? No, we prefer to take this much-abused cliché at face value and to denounce the Social Democratic Party's pretention to exclusivity: No, Willy Brandt, well disciplined as the Social Democratic Party of Germany may be, compliantly as it may bow to the autocratic dictate of a Herbert Wehner, you by yourself have no right to decide what Social Democracy means, what it can and should be. No more than Herr Ulbricht can claim to be the custodian of Marxist doctrine, no more than a Franz-Josef Strauss can claim the exclusive right to harness the Christian doctrine to his party cart, can you claim the exclusive right to speak for the party of August Bebel,[1] and now less than ever, since we have seen that Herbert Wehner *et al.* have no scruples about side-stepping the questions and demands of their comrades and subordinating everything else to tactical considerations.

I am not defending the Leftist or liberal splinter groups. On the contrary, my advice to you all is to come forward at every possible opportunity with party book in hand and demand an accounting. I fear that Herbert Wehner would be only too pleased to see little Leftist groups walk out of the party. In view of the 5 percent restrictive clause they would be politically ineffectual. If anything, they lend impetus to the N.P.D., which very soon may be able to take the 5 percent hurdle with ease.

---

[1] Associate of Wilhelm Liebknecht and one of the founders of the Social Democratic Party (1869); member of newly formed Reichstag (1871); died 1913.

The Christian Social Union nominated a candidate for the Chancellorship; with the votes of the C.S.U. and the C.D.U. this candidate defeated his rivals Schröder and Barzel. Kiesinger was a member of the National Socialist Party from 1933 to 1945. In other words, two parties that call themselves Christian have supported a man they shamelessly represent as a Resistance fighter, a man who as a fully responsible adult acted in a manner contrary to all Christian morality. This may be a matter of indifference to the C.D.U. and the C.S.U.; after all, these parties, under Konrad Adenauer, allowed themselves the luxury of a Hans Globke.

As the largest and most cohesive of the three coalition parties, the S.P.D. should have provided the Chancellor. It did not. It agreed, modestly and much too quickly, to Kiesinger. The Social Democratic Party is rightly proud of its history. It honors the memory of its murdered Resistance fighters. How, and with what false protestations, will it henceforth honor the memory of a Julius Leber or a Carlo Mierendorf [1]? The Social Democratic Party of Germany has, by a majority vote, permitted Franz-Josef Strauss to become a Minister again. We know the excuses. Allegedly he can more easily be kept under control; allegedly he could exert more power and do more harm as secretary of the C.D.U./C.S.U. parliamentary party. Such tactical hocus-pocus reminds one of 1933, when it was alleged that Adolf Hitler would very quickly run himself into the ground as Chancellor.

All three parties have made it very easy for the rapidly growing National Democratic Party to attract a flow of the underprivileged and of emotionally unstable malcontents. If a man who was a member of the National Socialist Party from 1933 to the surrender can today, with public approval, become Chancellor, it means that National Socialism has once more become respectable. The N.P.D. slogan "We can vote again" now has a twin

---

[1] Social Democrat, incarcerated by the Nazis and killed in prison during an air raid.

brother: "It's all right to have been a Nazi." And soon it will be taught in our history classes that a Minister can lie to the Parliament and nevertheless be reappointed.

And what now? The usual helplessness? Resigned inactivity, since the fellows on top do what they like anyway? The familiar pose: politics is and remains a dirty business? Thoughts of emigration and similar sentimentalities? No. We're going to stay right here. We are the state. We are not going to form splinter groups and walk out of the party. We are not going to sulk in the corner.

We will keep our eyes open and see what Kurt Georg Kiesinger and Herbert Wehner do to justify their impositions on us and on the state. The former's Nazi past and the latter's totalitarian practices are the dowry of the Great Coalition that went into effect on December 1st. We shall keep our eyes open and see whether Willy Brandt succeeds—even with the help of shifting majorities, in other words with the votes of the F.D.P.[1]—in putting through his united-Germany policy. . . . If the Great Coalition can boast no other activity than the issuing of emergency laws, we can only hope that it collapses before it brings about the collapse of the Federal Republic.

The S.P.D. has entered the government under the most questionable circumstances. The government's statement of aims will soon show whether the conscience of the S.P.D. operates also on the government bench.

[1] Freie Demokratische Partei—Free Democratic Party.

THE CITIZEN'S FIRST DUTY

*Address delivered at Hans-Sachs-Haus in Gelsenkirchen
on January 5, 1967, on the occasion of the opening of the
school year at the Gelsenkirchen School for Popular
Education.*

Ladies and gentlemen:

The "political landscape" is a conception dear to our richly
metaphoric language. From time to time a commentator informs
us—and the words often have a certain mystical ring—that our
"political landscape has changed." It did so in 1933. And then
amid the rubble heaps of 1945 the change was plain for all to
see. Anyone who still remembers the contrast between empty
shopwindows and suddenly overflowing shopwindows will have
to admit that our political landscape changed with the currency
reform. Unfortunately, very few of us realized to what extent rearmament would change not only our political, but our unpolitical landscape as well. Since the turn of the year, when the Great
Coalition was foisted on us, our versatile landscape has changed
again and, it is to be feared, will continue to change to a terrifying degree. Proportional administration,[1] a swiftly spreading

1 See note, p. 61.

72

virus disease, will creep into the most insignificant government office. The presence of a former Nazi in the Chancellery, however ingeniously he may try to represent himself as a Resistance fighter, will make National Socialism respectable again. Law No. 131[1] will exert a more decisive influence on our society than the Basic Law. Since I have children and you have children who are expected to grow up in this country, it is imperative that we relegate resignation to the vacation months and remind the citizen of his duties. My speech is therefore entitled "The Citizen's First Duty."

A citizen has the right to vote. This right is a direct tie between him and the state. A citizen pays taxes to the federal government and to the state; this is another tie between him and the state, which is something the state likes to forget, although it lives off the citizen and obligates him to pay taxes. Does the state, in addition to the obligation to pay taxes and to bear arms, impose other obligations on the citizen? In our schoolrooms it was already drummed into us that the citizen's first duty is docility. We recall that after the battle of Jena, after the collapse of Prussia, that museum of former glory, the commandant of Berlin proclaimed to the uneasy if not rebellious citizenry that the citizen's first duty was to keep calm; that not Prussia but the King had lost a battle. And that's been the story in Germany ever since. Germans have complied with the order to keep calm every time—for their benefit or at their expense—a battle has been lost on the Volga, an emergency law promulgated in the Reichstag, rearmament voted in the Parliament, their tax money squandered in an election campaign.

And yet considerable efforts have been made to install unrest as the citizen's first duty. From the inception of the German En-

---

[1] Law authorizing the payment of pensions to former members of the Nazi Party.

lightenment down to our own day the question has been debated with pedantic zeal: Is the citizen's first duty quiet or disquiet, rest or unrest, to keep calm or to get excited? A fit subject for high school essays. I can see a nineteen-year-old student—either in opposition to his teacher or with his benevolent encouragement—taking up cudgels for unrest. But then, once he has left the shelter of the classroom and turns his mind to such serious things as security and a neatly scheduled career, he puts unrest behind him as youthful folly and aligns himself with the party of order, calm and rest.

I should like to cite three examples to show how in this country great and justified unrest can be deflated into self-satisfied or resigned calm and complacency. When rearmament came up for discussion in the Parliament in 1954–55 and violent debates arose on the subject, an unrest based on the still evident consequences of the war gave rise to the "Count me out" movement. The survivors of the classes of 1918 to 1928 gave a simple nonpolitical answer to the question of rearmament. That answer, based exclusively on their own interest, was: "Count me out." The government knew just what to do. It exempted these sorely tried classes, which were decimated to begin with, and relied on the largely inexperienced younger age groups. The younger men did not say: "Count me out." They kept calm and played along.

As everyone knows, rearmament was put through over the opposition of the S.P.D. The "Count me out" movement died an inglorious death. For having said no, the Social Democrats were subjected to a nation-wide slander campaign, and two years later the C.D.U./C.S.U. under Konrad Adenauer won an absolute majority in the Parliament, a great victory for the precept that complacent calm is the citizen's first duty.

My second example of germinating and erupting unrest is the *Spiegel* affair. Neither Herr Strauss nor Herr Adenauer had expected such an outburst of public opinion. This great civic-spirited unrest even brought certain democratic results: the Parliament reacted; Strauss, who had lied to the Parliament, was obliged to resign. But now that momentary unrest has once again given way to a respectable calm, he is back in office. Only his haircut has been changed; and he speaks more softly: his credit rating has fallen.

Which brings us to my third example of unrest as the citizen's first duty: a few weeks ago when the threat of the Great Coalition appeared on the horizon, the postal service was kept busy. Telegrams were sent, letters were written; I sent some too. Democratic virtue made itself very audible and the S.P.D. had reason to be taken aback. But once the Great Coalition was an accomplished fact the S.P.D. drew up its balance sheet, and lo and behold, when the withdrawals from the party were checked off against new applications it turned out that the membership had increased.

And yet, ladies and gentlemen, we often hear of "German unrest" or "the restless Germans."

Anyone who travels frequently abroad has heard the anxious question: Why are Germans so restless; what makes them so restless? This "German unrest" is feared in France, Poland and England, in Czechoslovakia and Scandinavia.

The questioners are not referring to the unrest which I should like to see established in permanence as the citizen's first duty, but to the aimless and extravagant unrest which roams from North Cape to the Black Sea, which lyrically embraces the whole world and mystically descends to the "Mothers"; they are referring to an unrest which projects itself upon the starry heavens and dreams of bringing happiness to the world with a kiss.

This extravagant cosmic unrest has as its foundation an excess of calm, dreary complacency. In between, in the area of democracy, where vigilant unrest is so urgently needed, there is a gaping void. True, attempts are made now and then to populate this for us still new territory. Barely six weeks ago we witnessed an outbreak of justified unrest, argumentative unrest, when the Great

Coalition was decided upon. Will it remain a mere stirring, followed by another relapse into stupefied calm? And will this calm in turn, this stifling stagnation, breed cosmic unrest, that "German unrest" which is rightly feared by our neighbors?

The afflux of new members to the N.P.D. has its source in just such a stifling atmosphere. One man sits by the fireside for ten years, then suddenly he jumps up and wants to save the world. Another flunks his exams and therefore, quite logically, decides to become a politician. Still another never changes his shirt but clamors for public housecleaning. Young people—though only a small fraction of our once again restlessly roaming youth—are feeding on the resentments that find eager gardeners in that fertile no man's land. What then, in view of all our defeats and meager successes, is the citizen's first duty? "Look reality in the face" becomes an imperative. For it was not fate that played us a dirty trick; we did it ourselves. Everyone knows that we have repressed items of information that ought to be repeated to the saturation point:

1. In 1933 Adolf Hitler did not seize power out of the blue; he became Chancellor legally, with the support of broad sections of the population. His book *Mein Kampf* had been on the market for years. In it he defined his aims clearly. Anyone who could read, a well-read man like Kurt Georg Kiesinger, for instance, must have known what Hitler was up to. But from sheer fear of Communism the bourgeois camp, against its better judgment, supported Hitler; consequently the complicity of the bourgeois opportunists weighs more heavily in the balance than the obvious guilt of misled idealists who wished with Hitler's help to transform *petit bourgeois* dreams of power into world policy.

2. The development begun in 1933 led to the Second World War. For all the negligence of the European powers, especially England and France, during the Spanish Civil War and at the time of the Munich Pact; for all the blindness with which Poland, a year before its military defeat, enriched itself at the ex-

pense of occupied Czechoslovakia, all serious historians agree that the aggressor—that is, the Great German Reich—bears sole responsibility for the war, even though Franz-Josef Strauss, that ubiquitous dilettante, never wearies of expressing a contrary opinion to a grateful public.

3. The crimes committed in Germany and in German-dominated territories from 1933 to 1945 are historical facts. These included not only the usual spontaneous pogroms or war atrocities. For the first time in the history of mankind the systematic destruction of whole sections of the population was planned, organized and carried out. Since then our courts have convicted only the executants of criminal acts, the Bogers and Kaduks.[1] True, our tender-hearted language, so prone to neologisms, has coined the term *"Schreibtischmörder"* (desk murderer), yet Hans Globke, author of a commentary on the Nuremberg Laws, was permitted for more than a decade to help guide the destinies of the Federal Republic.

4. In May 1945 unconditional surrender put an end to the power-political hybris and the organized crime of the Great German Reich. For a few years ruins and hardship served as a reminder that we had lost the war.

5. The incorporation of the Federal Republic into the Western bloc and the conversion of a reconstruction effort in which every section of the population participated into an Economic Miracle soon submerged the general realization that the war had been lost. The consequences were disastrous. More and more a temporarily divided country was transformed into two hostile states. This development was intensified by West German rearmament and the resultant drastically anti-Communist "policy of strength," a policy whose sole result was to consolidate each of the two German states and to exacerbate the breach between them. Such a policy is obsolete. Even if the coalition government

---

[1] Subordinate concentration camp guards recently brought to trial.

has managed to bring the foreign and domestic policies of the Federal Republic into line with the momentary political state of the world, this can hardly be called an achievement; it is merely an obvious step that was long overdue.

But what is the present situation of the two German states?

The three Western victorious powers gave their occupation zones a fair chance; they made it possible for West Germany to regenerate in a short time as a democratic state with an exemplary constitution. The D.D.R., on the other hand, was not so fairly treated by its protector and occupying power. Reparations payments and the dismantling of factories impeded its economic development. It was only after Stalin's death that slowly, with interruptions and relapses, the miniature economic miracle of East Germany began. While in the Federal Republic the "restorationists," with the help of an ideological anti-Communism, were watering down our democracy, the D.D.R. was dashing the hopes set in it by the Communist camp: apart from Albania, the D.D.R. is the only neo-Stalinist state in Europe.

Whereas after 1956 the bordering countries, Poland and Czechoslovakia, at varying speeds, sometimes rushing ahead of the Soviet Union, sometimes by emulation, surpassed it, sought their individual anti-Stalinist road to socialism and to some extent found it, East Germany clung to its Stalinist despotism. Over the years, it built up an army which derived its inspiration from Prussian militarism, while its youth organization, the Free German Youth, came more and more to resemble the Hitler Youth. This political petrifaction had similar consequences in both German states: just as the Federal Republic is isolated within its system of alliances, so the D.D.R. is isolated within the Warsaw Pact, and presumably hated as well. It is hardly to be expected that the neighbors of either of these states will be very eager to unite two such obstructive and incalculable allies.

6. What can we do to encourage our Eastern neighbors to facilitate the first steps, if not toward reunification then at least

toward a gradual *rapprochement* between the two states? I believe that our side should attempt to obtain a peace treaty and put forward clear proposals to that end. The time has come for us to state plainly and without evasions what is obvious to all: that regardless of how the German state is federated or confederated, its Eastern border can only be the Oder-Neisse line. Since we were responsible for a war which displaced first Poland's Eastern border and then our own Eastern border, it is incumbent on us to accept and recognize this development. Our second proposal should be the disarmament of both German states—a solution for which we should seek the approval of the four victorious powers. The Federal Republic must take the first step.

7. If we concede that only a government upheld by a Great Coalition can be strong enough to make such decisions, then we must also demand that the Great Coalition government now in power should demonstrate its justification by doing what no previous government has dared to do. If in the next three years our government does not draw the conclusions that follow from our loss of the war, if it does not obtain a peace treaty establishing our internal and external borders by agreement with our neighbors to the East and the West, the Great Coalition, for all the success it may achieve in minor matters, will have wasted its opportunity and fallen short of its duty.

So much for the duties of the state. But who is the state? Is it the governing parties plus the opposition which according to the Basic Law shares in the responsibility of government? The citizen too is a part of the state and should—this is the beginning of his responsibility—regard himself as a part of the state. How is this possible if in increasing degree politics is taken to mean power politics, if power reacts only to power, if consciously or unconsciously our political life is conditioned by Stalin's question: "How many divisions has the Pope?" Indeed, the individual citizen has his vote, but isn't the choice narrowed down from year to year? Has this vote still any real weight, or has it ceased to be anything more than the ornament of a purely formal democracy which in content is becoming more and more Portuguese, a development encouraged by our inborn penchant for the authoritarian state? I cannot answer these questions. But if you are prepared to honor unrest as the citizen's first duty, the citizen will be the first power in the state and will find an answer.

What can be done concretely, that is, here and now? Here in the Ruhr many citizens have helped for years to build up the unions and the Social Democratic Party of Germany. I suggest that all of you—each for himself—call on those democratic organizations which share responsibility for the government to do their duty. Demand, and keep demanding, that they respect the will expressed by your vote. Take care that the amorphous condition of other parties does not spread to the Socialist Party. Appeal to the candidates you have elected to follow their own conscience rather than party pressures. Continue to be restless and difficult. The citizen's first duty is unrest.

THE PINPRICK SPEECH

Delivered before the League of the Victims of Political, Racial and Religious Persecution, Berlin, January 29, 1967.

Ladies and gentlemen:

We are in danger of losing nothing less than our rights as adult citizens. So it's too late to worry about upsetting potted plants or stepping on people's toes. It is time to call not only our opponents but ourselves as well to account, undeterred by the usual fear of being applauded by the wrong camp or the likelihood that our words will be distorted by the Springer press. What is the occasion of this meeting? The eve of January 30th? Shall we once again make a solemn ritual of the paralyzed immobility in which the cunning little bunny rabbit waits for the snake to strike?

Anyone who sees us sitting here, divided in matters of detail but all goaded by the ambition to be Lefter than Left or in any case Left in an original way, and all saturated with knowledge of the old Left, the new Left, and the missing Left; anyone who sees us sitting here, impotent but in some degree relishing our impo-

tence; anyone who sees us sitting here in Berlin, far away from
the winegrowers of the Palatinate, the idiosyncrasies of the Dit-
marsh peasants and the political vigor of the beer hall mobs of
Franconia—anyone who sees us sitting here like this at a time
when the N.P.D. is on the rise might well be filled with alarm,
not because of the N.P.D. but because of the impression we make
on him: we look so dignified; something must be wrong. So much
honest endeavor, so much dogmatic knowledge, so much Leftist
solemnity and so little of the gusto it would take to upset our well-
tempered desks—if only for a time—and rush out into the exhausting richness, variety and contradiction of everyday life.

I understand you, I understand us; it is a pleasure for one who
is seldom understood to find friends with unimpaired memories
and carloads of quotations who are talented enough to call their
own wretched situation by its name. The outsiders. Our aura of
virile melancholy sits becomingly on us. We have always known
it. This was bound to happen. No one listened to us. We are the
last antifascists.

What is an antifascist?

Whoever may have invented this cliché, there have been and
still are people who have it perpetually on their lips if not on
their letterheads. Is the word "antifascist" a trade-mark? Since a
cliché means everything and nothing, Walter Ulbricht and Karl
Jaspers, Herr von Thadden[1] and Pastor Niemöller are all antifascists. Let us forgo the badge. It is too easy to counterfeit and
mass-produce, its bearers are legion. Even Kurt Georg Kiesinger
is an antifascist. We have seen how, not without elegance, he
hesitated when in addition to the Chancellorship he was bidden
to assume the alas so difficult task of reconciling the German
people (can that have meant fascists and antifascists?). Kurt
Georg Kiesinger feels free from guilt, and since, as I am inclined
to believe, he was never actually a convinced National Socialist

---

[1] Adolf von Thadden, leader of the National Democrats.

but rather an opportunistic fellow traveler, it cannot have been hard for him to acquit himself.

Our laws apply to the actual perpetrators of criminal acts. Thus de-Nazification, an absurdity as it has operated up to now, has affected only the petty block leader, the SS-Untersturmführer (lieutenant) and the corner grocer. In our courts Auschwitz has been reduced to such cases as Boger and Kaduk. Such inner antifascists as Hans Globke and Kurt Georg Kiesinger were enabled by their higher positions to arm themselves with lily-white certificates for every eventuality.

Ladies and gentlemen: I make this speech reluctantly. Nowadays anyone who points to the self-evident in this country is suspected of wanting to shatter taboos, of being a wrong-headed disturber of the peace. The leading parties have closed their ranks to such a degree that the space between them offers no room for leverage; at the most a fine pin can be driven into the interstices. Call this "The Pinprick Speech" if you like. It's all right with me as long as it hurts.

I can already hear them: "These grumblers, know-it-alls and wet blankets. No sooner do we get a new Chancellor than they find a hair in the soup. See here—what have you got against Kiesinger? The man repented of his error. And besides he has merit."

If he were not the Chancellor I should find it easy to like Herr Kiesinger. He functions on so many levels that Thomas Mann might have invented him. There was nothing but the political alternative offered by the Social Democrats to prevent one from regarding Kurt Georg Kiesinger as a candidate acceptable to many Swabians. But without wishing to make a criterion of my Hanseatic origin and West Prussian upbringing, I cannot help saying that Baden-Württemberg is no more the Federal Republic than Saxony is synonymous with East Germany. In other words, what may, with a certain indulgence and in view of the large number of Protean careers, be acceptable in Stuttgart, ought not to have been possible in Bonn.

On November 30, 1966, I wrote a letter (since other avenues of protest were denied me) to the then premier of the *Land* of Baden-Württemberg, calling his attention to the consequences of his decision.[1] To this letter I have still received no answer. In *Civis* (January 1967), a monthly close to the Youth Union and hence to the Christian Democrats, Heinrich Vormweg[2] takes the view that in the eyes of the provincial Premier and future Chancellor my letter was merely the expression of a private opinion and therefore without importance. I quote: "Nevertheless both the letter and the demand expressed in it called for an answer. For very pertinent reasons. Kiesinger's membership in the National Socialist Party is undoubtedly a sensitive point for the present government of the Federal Republic, not only for reasons of foreign policy but in principle as well. The matter was discussed behind closed doors during the negotiations leading to the coalition. This may satisfy a good many people, because in this instance the Social Democratic Party may pass for a father confessor whose absolution merits blind confidence. This absolution in itself is not sufficient. In any case a number of intellectuals are far from satisfied with it."

And elsewhere Vormweg writes:

"Conceivably there are good reasons why Kiesinger disregarded his handicap and why the big parties backed him up. The one thing that seems inadmissible, especially in view of this candidacy and this Chancellorship, is to have withheld the matter from public view."

We can assume that Heinrich Vormweg's comment will also strike the Chancellor as a private opinion without importance and will remain unanswered. One is tempted of course to criticize Herr Kiesinger's manners, but where would that get us? If we are troubled today, it's not over Herr Kiesinger's breeding. The truth

---

[1] See p. 65.
[2] German literary critic.

of the matter is that the justified protests of innumerable citizens could not have meant anything to Kurt Georg Kiesinger. For once again . . . no clear distinction is made between a political decision and a just decision. A political decision was made, and we who are old-fashioned enough to advocate just decisions were accused of touching naïveté, though given credit for a sincere albeit misled patriotism. "You simply don't understand anything about politics. That's how it's always been in politics. Like it or not, politics has to apply different standards. Occasionally morality draws the short end. Don't worry so much, be optimistic. Write your books. You're doing all right, aren't you? It all gets published, doesn't it?"

Yes, to be sure, it still gets published. However, permit me a few more questions: Can a man who has forged checks become Chancellor?—Never.

Can a man who has been declared the guilty party in a divorce suit become Chancellor?—Unthinkable.

Can a Nazi become Chancellor?—If he has repented, yes, certainly.

Then can a forger who has repented of his forgery become Chancellor?

The theater of the absurd has opened its doors to a new company, the government. Where only the night before Ionesco was piling up his chairs, new actors have gone to work. A political troupe has undertaken to give us the shudders. . . .

But what is Herr Kiesinger's special merit? A man who opposed National Socialism both before and after 1933 deserves respect. Such merit was within the reach of a Willy Brandt, endowed as he was with a certain capacity for reasoning and with an innate sense of political morality. To him it was obvious what his conduct should be. Herr Kiesinger had a much harder time of it. He had to pass through error and delusion. But didn't German idealism hallow such error? Hasn't his striving for the good, the beautiful and the absurd led him out of the Purgatory of error?

He is the true Resistance fighter. Anybody is capable of knowing what is right and acting accordingly, but to go astray, to fall and nevertheless to land butter side up, that is an achievement and deserves its reward.

You will have noticed, ladies and gentlemen, that I am not prepared to give the Great Coalition government the usual fair chance. This is not a football field; there is no referee ready to blow his whistle when he sees a foul. This meeting, as the poster announces, is devoted to the "Menace from the Right," but I see no point in garnishing it with references to the mounting success of the National Democratic Party. What can we say to an addled young law student who falls for a freshly incubated and still shamefaced Rightist extremism, if the monstrous fact that a former Nazi like Kurt Georg Kiesinger can become a Chancellor is accepted with hardly a murmur by all the parties represented in the Parliament, not to mention the public?

The 8 percent of the electorate who vote for the National Democrats are not a serious danger to the Federal Republic. No. But the unconstitutional degradation of the highest government offices will undermine the health of our young and fragile democracy. In 1945 we lost a war; on December 1, 1966, the Federal Republic lost the peace, capitulating in regard to both the past and the future. But it is not Herr Kiesinger and Herr Wehner who will have to pay for this new capitulation; it is we who will foot the bill, we who are told with a pat on the back that we are too young to take a sound view of the troubled times before and after 1933.

Yet, surprisingly enough, the younger generation in our country are not yet aware of the burdens they will have to bear from this time on. We may have imported certain patterns of behavior and misbehavior from the United States of America, but the vigilance of the American younger generation toward their President has not been sufficiently emulated in our country. Only a few weeks ago student committees representing over a hundred

American universities made it unmistakably clear to President Johnson that he, his government and the soldiers who obeyed his orders were coming more and more to resemble the war criminals who had been condemned to death in Nuremberg in 1945. Energetically but without hysteria the American students have spoken out for democracy. Their words have struck home: under the pressure of the Pope's increasingly urgent appeals and of the vigilant young people of his country, President Johnson will have to make up his mind. He will go down in history as a man who has extended the list of the world's war crimes and gambled away the moral credit of his country.

But let's stick to our own back yard: How do our young people react when the substance of our democracy is openly vitiated? How do our young people react here and now when the millions who were murdered or whose lives were shattered because they tried to resist are once more insulted by the installation of a former Nazi as Chancellor? They have demonstrated and protested with enthusiasm and perseverance. There are plenty of pretexts for making these protest actions ineffectual by splitting them. Anyone who is preparing to make his entrance on the political scene in the shadow of Herr Kiesinger will find it relatively easy, after a careful study of the behavior of our protesting youth, to enthrone himself and his political plans.

Ladies and gentlemen, I doubt if you have expected any comfort from me. I cannot offer you any rosy hopes. I myself have reason to doubt the effectiveness of my speech. I know that many who today contemplate one or the other Germany with alarm and who, gathered together with their friends in the late melancholy hours, deplore the gravity of the situation, will tomorrow accept the Federal Cross of Merit from the hands of the man who still shows no misgivings about remaining our Chancellor. After fighting down a certain reluctance they will find it possible to participate in the councils of Herr Kiesinger. From what I know of our citizens' unstinting loyalty to the government, any government, they will stifle their occasional feelings of having fallen into bad company under the comforting reflection that the issue is not Herr Kiesinger or Herr Lübke,[1] but something bigger— peace, freedom and democracy—that their true motivation is concern for the fate of their brothers and sisters in the other Germany.

No. The most I can expect of this speech is that it will begin to puncture a widespread self-deception. For here in this country a mistaken sense of loyalty heaps late blessings on yesterday's crime; three decades later the opportunism of the thirties is rewarded. Here in this country only disobedience can save democracy. I call on those who wish to combat the danger on the Right effectively, those who are devoted to a country that still has a breathing chance of offering a democratic alternative to the old Stalinist dictatorship, to resist Herr Kiesinger, and not to make common cause with Herr Lübke. I call on them to act as a brake and a dam, in order that we may avoid having to blush for our country once again, and to fight for the day, however distant, when we shall be able to speak of our country without blushing.

[1] Second President of the West German Republic, successor to Theodor Heuss.

BEN AND DIETER:
A SPEECH TO THE ISRAELIS

Delivered in Tel Aviv and Jerusalem in early 1967, on the occasion of a trip to Israel.

While I was writing this paper, the German Social Democrat, Fritz Erler, died. A country that has always followed the wrong models has lost a model man. When the German middle classes succumbed to National Socialism in 1933—often against their better judgment—the high school student Fritz Erler said: "No." And stuck by it. This man who scorned ambiguity dared to resist, at a time when many others sought the refuge of "inner emigration." At twenty-five he was brought to trial and jailed. In the spring of 1945 escape saved him from transfer to Dachau.

I'm bound to the country I come from by background and language, the obligations of tradition and historical sins, by love and hate.

I was born in Danzig in 1927. At fourteen I was a Hitler Youth; at sixteen a soldier, and at seventeen an American prisoner of war. These dates meant a great deal in an era that purposefully slaughtered one year's crop of young men, branded the next year's crop with guilt, and spared another. You can tell by the date of my birth that I was too young to have been a Nazi but old enough to have been molded by a system that, from 1933 to 1945, at first surprised, then horrified, the world. The man who is speaking to you, then, is neither a proven antifascist nor an ex-National Socialist, but rather the accidental product of a crop of young men who were either born too early or infected too late. Innocent through no merit of my own, I became part of a postwar period that was never to be a period of real peace. Today, at thirty-nine, I occasionally have talks with eighteen-year-olds. They feel —twenty-two years after the unconditional surrender—that their fathers left them a bad mortgage and they can't understand why they're being asked to pay it off.

The young people of my country are no better and no worse than the young people of other countries. With understandable egotism they want to make a fresh start without having to be marked men, without having to drag the ballast of guilt into their futures. A number of friendly adjectives can be applied to the young people of my country as appropriately as to those anywhere else: they are outgoing, polite, ready to help, eager to discuss things; and even relaxed, unless they are forced to speak as representatives of a Germany they never knew. Some of these young people have made the adjustment to their circumstances, the great adjustment that levels everything. Poorly taught, and while in school still hard pressed by the demands made on them both inside and outside Germany, more and more of these young people take refuge in political indifference or in protest that is politically indifferent.

Heretical though my thesis may sound, it is entirely possible for a twenty-year-old student to venerate, in her little room, the photograph and memory of Anne Frank and yet, confused by the contradictions of reality, go out the next day and vote for a party that only barely camouflages its readiness to step into the boots of the National Socialist Party. How can a twenty-year-old girl be expected to recognize symptoms of Nazi revival in this aspiring party of the radical Right, when an early member of the National Socialist Party is allowed to hold the Chancellorship today in my country? Why should she reject Mr. von Thadden's nationalism when Christian politicians, spurred by occasional opportunism, try to top Mr. von Thadden's neo-nationalistic hybris? How difficult is it for young people growing up to remain reasonable in the blare of such political gangster jargon, and make political decisions based on political reason? I say reason, although I know that all appeals to reason are but flickerings on a TV set which has had its sound switched off. We are still holding forth, but our listeners' ears have grown to tunnels; not a single word sticks. We don't talk past each other; we talk right through each other. Do you still know what I'm saying, when I say reason? No? Then I'll try a story.

My story is called BEN AND DIETER.

I can see them clearly, doing their laundry in red American army gasoline. Their voices tangle in quarrels, in laughter. Ben and Dieter did exist. I observed them during the summer of 1945 at the Fürstenfeldbruck air base in southern Germany. I watched them skillfully and systematically swipe American K-rations to sell on the black market. Before they could function as a team, a getting-acquainted period was necessary, because neither man saw an accomplice in the other, at first. A third person was required, a catalyst.

Dieter and Ben—or Ben and Dieter—were seventeen at the time. Ben had survived the Theresienstadt concentration camp and Dieter, a soldier at sixteen, had, without knowing quite how, survived Rundstedt's Ardennes offensive. Ben lived in a displaced-persons camp: he was a DP. Dieter lived in an American prisoner-of-war camp near Fürstenfeldbruck. He was a prisoner of war.

Both groups, the DP's and the POW's, worked at the Fürstenfeldbruck air base in the spacious barracks that Hermann Göring had built for the Great German Air Force. Dieter, who was still

close to his school days, served as an interpreter for a small group
of POW's who were put to work as dishwashers in an American
army kitchen. His school English became more and more colored
with the kitchen slang of the American army cooks. Ben, in a DP
group, worked for the same outfit. He was in charge of the laundry room and pressed the well-cut trousers and shirts of American
soldiers, who, smartly dressed, relaxed and armed with small presents, would go fraternizing in Fürstenfeldbruck and Landsberg
on the Lech. It was unavoidable—and it was not avoided:
Dieter's kitchen squad and Ben's laundry boys clashed during the
short break after meals behind the complex dishwashing appa-
ratus of the American army: the garbage can, the soapy-water can
and the chlorine-rinse can. Adolescent former concentration-
camp inmates and adolescent former soldiers whose uniforms still
showed the outlines of the Nazi eagles that had been removed.
Their fighting amused the American kitchen bosses. Their hatred
was blind, single-tracked, always in the same direction. Both
groups spoke camp and barracks German: "Spread your cheeks!
Line up on the man in front of you! You jerks!" No matter how
each had survived the system, it was the same system that had
molded them both. In addition to a company dog that also lived
off the kitchen, the outfit for which both boys worked in ex-
change for exotic-tasting meals kept a kind of cultural attaché, a
lieutenant named Hermann Mautler, nearsighted and about
thirty, who had been allowed to leave Vienna with his parents
still in time, in 1938. Mautler was a historian. He had studied at
Princeton and returned to Europe with the American army. He
believed in his field, in enlightenment and in reason. He tried to
put a stop to Ben's emotional outbursts and to Dieter's instinctive
aggressions by explaining their motivations to them. Much to the
delight of the American kitchen bosses, we see him rush into the
melee. We see him administer enlightenment. He assembles both
groups on the sunny lawn in front of the barracks building. We
listen to him speak with intelligence, modesty and little under-

standing of the situation. Ben and Dieter are not interested in what he has to say. Ben says: "Turn off the speech, man." And Dieter prefers the clover in the grass to Hermann Mautler's education. He is looking for a four-leaf clover; Ben is telling jokes with sinister punch lines thought up in the camp at Theresienstadt; Hermann Mautler tries and tries. His is the boring, laborious task of reasoning. Step by step he wants to analyze Ben's route to the concentration camp for him; he wants to demonstrate to Dieter for what criminal purposes he has been schooled, and by what means.

The man of reason achieves a peculiar success: Ben and Dieter stop fighting; they unite against Mautler. The system to which their young minds and their language were subjected is still effective. Ben and Dieter cut into the middle of Mautler's skillfully prepared speech on "Anti-Semitism in German Schools and Universities," bursting out with the song: "O you lovely Westerwald." Ben had been forced to memorize and sing the German soldiers' song in the concentration camp; Dieter grew an inch taller while learning to sing the song on the troop training grounds at Fallingbostel. Hermann Mautler doesn't know the song, but he's heard of the Westerwald. Diplomatically he tries to bridge this gap in his education, asks to be filled in, and gets laughed at: "What a jerk! Doesn't even know 'O you lovely Westerwald' and goes around making speeches!" But Hermann Mautler isn't ready to give up. For two more weeks he continues trying to administer his education: for two more weeks he talks into the sometimes hummed, sometimes roared words of the Westerwald song. He makes a few desperate efforts to win over his pupils by joining in the song: "O you lovely Westerwald/ Cold whistles the wind across your heights so bald. . . ."

I want to remember exactly. Ben and Dieter hated Hermann Mautler. They hated his superiority. They hated his skillfully diplomatic attempts at effacing this superiority. They hated him because he had been molded by a different system—the name "Princeton" became an insult. They hated him because he was right; right all the time. To Ben and Dieter, Mautler was the "adult," and anybody who had survived Theresienstadt or the Ardennes offensive at seventeen hated adults. I don't know whether Hermann Mautler finally gave up, or not. The dissolution of the POW and DP camps saved him from total defeat. Dieter was released from the prisoner-of-war camp. Ben found passage on a freighter to Israel. Today, both are gentlemen of forty, married, fathers of children. They have a profession and still a good bit of life left to live.

Can we be absolutely sure that Hermann Mautler—and with him reason—was defeated at the Fürstenfeldbruck air base? I'm not sure. Reason does not wage blitzkriegs; its campaigns are not followed by instant victory. Reason operates slowly. Hermann Mautler's fight against ignorance has stayed with me although at the time I understood him no better than Ben and Dieter did.

What was Mautler's isolation made of? If I remember accurately, it was his assignment to "take care of the cultural needs" of two American companies, one including Negro soldiers, the other exclusively white. We—meaning Ben's and Dieter's groups—saw the hatred between white and black soldiers fan out in tiny particles over their day-to-day lives. Why should we be different? We, at least, had one thing in common: "O you lovely Westerwald." Hermann Mautler stood apart from any group. He wasn't black and he was too intelligent to take refuge in his position as a white man. Of course he knew how Theresienstadt had come into being and about the crimes that sixteen- and seventeen-year-olds had been the victims of right up to the last days of the war, but he couldn't join in the singing of "O you lovely Westerwald," and when he did, it sounded wrong: we sensed his educational intent.

What did Hermann Mautler do wrong? Was he not a good enough teacher? Every word he said was right. Only one thing stood in his way: blind, amoral reality with its primal demands. I remember that while Mautler preached enlightenment and reason Ben could think of nothing but neckties, fashionable colors, stripes and dots with bold-checkered jackets and herringbone trousers. The title of his passion was: I want to wear civilian clothes. I don't want to hear anything. Why can't he shut up about his Weimar Republic? I want to wear silk shirts.

And Dieter could think of nothing but a girl who walked past at noon every day on her way to her job with an American outfit. Dieter had never been to bed with a girl.

Is this the end of my story? Has it emphasized a special case and made it more interesting than it actually was? This story can be continued and varied. There were once two wise old statesmen who carried out their political designs forcefully and sometimes ruthlessly. One was named David Ben-Gurion, the other Konrad Adenauer. Both thought they came from those good old times long before the crime. That made them conservative and enabled them to become friends. But one old man had a capable, hardworking, inconspicuous aide among his supporters whom, for conservative reasons, he did not wish to give up; and his friend Ben-Gurion could understand this. But people in Konrad Adenauer's country and in David Ben-Gurion's country said: "What! The Hans Globke who is helping Adenauer run the country is the same Hans Globke who wrote the commentaries to the Nuremberg race laws, who helped prepare the murder of six million people."

Objections to Hans Globke were voiced loudly and softly, violently and calmly, in great detail, accusingly. None of this disturbed old man Adenauer, nor did old Ben-Gurion want to abandon his friendship with Konrad Adenauer. So all of us had to get adjusted to the idea of Hans Globke and his partnership with Konrad Adenauer, the same Konrad Adenauer who was David Ben-Gurion's friend.

Since, however, getting adjusted to political crimes gives license for new crimes, I ask myself: "Were the two old men any more intelligent or reasonable than Ben and Dieter? Will this story go on forever? Will reason, as represented by Hermann Mautler at the Fürstenfeldbruck air base, by the Social Democrat Adolf Arndt in the German Parliament, always be defeated because Ben and Dieter didn't want to give up their 'lovely Westerwald'? Because Ben-Gurion doesn't want his friendship with another old man broken off on account of a Hans Globke? Is this how history is made?" It would seem that our history, at least, is made this way.

A man from one of the two Germanys comes and tells you a story. Why does he tell stories instead of exhorting you to seek reconciliation, brotherhood and penance? Because he doesn't want to auction off the shopworn goods that stand in our showcases today, dusty and pathetic like old marksmanship cups and athletic trophies.

It is too late to call upon our consciences. Twenty-two years after the spread of mankind's greatest crime was brought to a halt by the unconditional surrender of the Great German Reich, adjustment to the crime is spreading. It has become a chapter in a schoolbook, a subject at the mercy of history teachers.

I come from a country in which an undercurrent of restoration is beginning to show itself openly. I come from one of the two Germanys—we do have two—each of which is still denying the other. Nevertheless, shouldn't we be satisfied and praise this inoffensive nation, which is still obediently accepting the effective control of the victorious powers, for its economic and cultural achievements? The catalogue of our accomplishments can brighten the booths at any fair. There was plenty of applause to help the German economic miracle, the miracle of reconstruction, the girl-and-football miracle, make headlines. I don't mean to be purely ironical about our achievements. My country is worthy of praise. And if you asked what makes it lovable and livable for me, I could praise it without getting loud about it. But I did not come here to praise all kinds of minor achievements—besides, there is no shortage in either country of loud-voiced soapbox orators preaching neo-German greatness.

The defeated and destroyed Germany showed the world what the world knew anyway: that the Germans can be an efficient people. But was that enough? Have we at long last succeeded in winning peace after a second lost war? Have we blotted out the dread of the negative side of our efficiency from the minds of our neighbors to the East and West? Have we been able to convince them that desire for revenge has not taken root among us, that Nazi revival, underground or above, will be checked, that our imperialism lies buried in the Caucasus and on the North Cape? After almost two decades of stupid and schizoid foreign policy the two Germanys are isolated within their systems of alliance, notwithstanding the stereotyped declamations of loyalty from both sides. We are viewed with suspicion and cautious respect. Our inability to find peace, state beside state, Germany beside Germany, will eventually exhaust the patience of our neighbors, if not today, then tomorrow.

And what can be said on the positive side? Our language has an idiom: "to foul one's own nest." It is often used as a political insult, for instance to describe analytical TV programs or criticism which lack a "constructive" element. Even this talk about adjustment to political crimes will be described as "fouling one's own nest" as soon as it reaches the readers of the Federal Republic. Because I have neglected to sing about the "lovely Westerwald." Since I refused to ride utopian hobbyhorses my speech has not been about reconciliation and brotherhood. I have spoken of the loss of Fritz Erler. I have spoken of Hermann Mautler's defeat. Two men on the treadmill of reason have been my models.

Because reason is my sole concern. It stands helpless in a world of increasing adjustment. It needs help, your help too. Do you understand me?

Translated by Helen Mustard, Venable Herndon,
and Ursule Molinaro

OBITUARY OF
AN OPPONENT

Published in Der Stern, *Hamburg, May 8, 1967.*

Konrad Adenauer is dead.

For many days he forced us to witness his dying.

We paused, each in his place; we counted backward until we ran into ruins, we tried to count forward in a world where he is no longer a point of reference.

We took leave of Konrad Adenauer while he was still dying; for years we had secretly rehearsed taking our leave of him and his much-wrinkled face.

Really of him? Or were we trying to take leave of a picture, the partial view of himself that he had seen fit to show us?

Was Konrad Adenauer in his last years still a person, or was he already the afterglow of an era that had been named for him? Still sly and capable of occasional participation in political intrigue, he was a burden to his unloved successor and a stumbling block to the mutually hostile crown princes.

His death embarrasses us.

Since there will be no lack of obituaries inspired solely by his greatness, we ask ourselves, I ask myself: How does a political opponent take leave of Konrad Adenauer?

Should he keep silent and let the laurel-twining panegyrists monopolize the occasion?

I believe that Konrad Adenauer deserved to be shown critical respect by his opponents.

He, the dry ascetic without vanity, always a man of ready and often cutting wit, would in any event have admonished the overly pompous to stick to the facts; he cannot possibly like it when his proselytes run his greatness into the ground.

How great was Konrad Adenauer? So great that he will soon stand enormously in our way? There is no absolute standard for the greatness of statesmen. Metternich's greatness gives us a yardstick for Adenauer's greatness; both statesmen, by their energy and talent, brought about a restoration.

We tend to say of a great statesman that he deserved well of his country, but we are seldom troubled by the question of what we mean by our country. What did Konrad Adenauer mean by his country?

Did he, who tenaciously pursued a policy of strength, really deserve well of his divided country or only of the Western half of his country?

On May 5, 1955, Konrad Adenauer signed the Paris Treaty. Speaking on the radio in a voice that gave more emphasis to Rhenish dialect than to the substance of his sentences, he read the "Proclamation of the Federal Republic to the German people on the day of the recovery of national sovereignty."

Combated by his opponents as the "Chancellor of the Allies," he, the guideline Chancellor, laid down rails that are still leading us into dead ends; from that moment on, the word "reunification" was not worth the paper on which it figured in election leaflets and Sunday declamations.

Anyone who wants to dismantle those rails will have to demolish Konrad Adenauer's political achievement.

His political achievement consisted in systematically consolidating the provisional part-state and turning it into a sovereign Federal Republic; rearmament was a by-product of this process.

In Walter Ulbricht, Konrad Adenauer found a congenial counterpart: two statesmen went fifty-fifty; their work is done.

Since the age of twenty-two I have found myself up against Konrad Adenauer's dogmatic will. His solitary decisions devaluated the political conceptions of my generation before they were formulated; he taught us the practice of helplessness; we adapted ourselves.

The chancellor democracy which developed in the shadow of his person revived a time-worn authoritarianism and incorporated the most conflicting interests into a political force under the trademark of The Christian Democratic Union.

Everything he did and accomplished was centered on himself. He recognized no opponents; his dogma, anti-Communism, permitted him to regard every opponent as an enemy. His opponents lacked his stature. His supporters lack his stature.

He spoke frankly, clairvoyantly and bluntly of his successor's incapacity.

He was not given to sentimentality. We know of only one utterance in which he reached out beyond the matter in hand and took refuge in pathos. In the summer of 1954, after the first disaster of the European Defense Community, Konrad Adenauer was heard to invoke the heavenly powers: "My God, what will become of Germany when I am gone?"

It would be a mistake to put this utterance down as megalomania. For Konrad Adenauer, Germany was reduced to the Federal Republic; this separate Germany was his work and hence identical with his implement, the C.D.U. majority. In this hour we shall do well to delete respectfully the higher authority invoked by Adenauer and interpret his utterance as follows: What is to become of the C.D.U. when Konrad Adenauer is gone?

For though the future may well teach us to reduce his political achievement to the consolidation of the Federal Republic, one thing is certain: Konrad Adenauer as the creator of a party dominated by himself was an outstanding figure; he was a great party chief.

For all the ambitious stepfathers the Christian Democrats may choose, his death leaves them orphaned. Father figures are not made to order.

Konrad Adenauer's term in office was distinguished by a continuous series of partial successes, and here the word "partial" should be taken in its double meaning: his successes benefited only one part of the country; the other part paid for them. His European goal remained a utopia.

But all criticism aside, his trip to Moscow will remain an enduring success, all the more so as it was followed, years later, by the aged Chancellor's rather startling observation: The Soviet Union is a peace-loving country.

In 1967 the nineteenth-century patriarch reluctantly took his leave of political life. We look around us and perceive to our consternation the innumerable revisions and delete signs which the ascetic will of an old man has left in our once youthful plan of building a democratic new Germany to succeed war, crime and dictatorship.

Now that the stern father is gone, it remains for us to come of age lest his work, his concept of a separate state, should survive us.

Left behind in his partial work, we look for an example with which to compare such long-drawn-out dying.

Let me tell you about the death of Lord Chamberlain Brigge as recorded in Rainer Maria Rilke's *Notebooks of Malte Laurids Brigge.* That strong-willed nobleman, accustomed to power, died for two whole months, screaming all the while. Groans and screams were said to have been heard long after his death in the Lord Chamberlain's castle of Ulsgaard.

Konrad Adenauer left us quietly and matter-of-factly, as though not wishing to disturb the political developments that are beginning, cautiously at first, to pierce doors and windows in his all-too-solid and lightless edifice of state.

But of Konrad Adenauer as of Chamberlain Brigge it may be said:

He died his own death.

PROVISIONAL BALANCE

Attempt at an Epilogue. Berlin, September 1967.

Hegel made the world a fatal gift in acquainting it with the world spirit. A nation which embodies the necessary factor in the dialectical content of history is the dominant nation, of which Hegel says: "Against its absolute right to be the vehicle of the world spirit's present state of development, the spirits of other nations are without rights, and, like those nations whose era is past, they no longer count in history." Hegel's philosophy has had consequences. Both Bismarck and Marx took from it what their dominant nation or dominant class required, and when systems of state power had taken shape in accordance with a vulgarized conception of Hegel, Stalin and Hitler became, consciously or unconsciously, disciples of Hegel. Under their rule, absolutist states were murderously refined into systems of state terror which differed almost diametrically in their ideological and national substance, resembled one another in their equation of party and state, and were identical in their missionary claims to power. But the influence of Hegel has continued even after Hitler and Stalin, all the more so as his exegetes coyly overlook the praxis of Hitler and Stalin, which they find embarrassing: nevertheless, the crushing of the Budapest uprising more than ten years ago as well as the American commitment in Vietnam can be laid to Hegel's doctrine of the power state. For in holding that it has been chosen to "liberate" the Vietnamese people, the United States believes itself to be inhabited by the world spirit. Heller's observation of 1921 is still timely: "Not only when philosophers speculate about the power state, but also whenever very practical power politics requires ideological gloss, it still derives that ideological gloss, often unconsciously, from Hegel."

This bondage to Hegel unites an otherwise disunited world. . . . Did Hegel desire this? Did Nietzsche wish—as Heidegger wished, though he never succeeded—to be taken literally by a Hitler? It is unfair to Hegel and Nietzsche to judge them by vulgarizations of their theses. But anyone who looks for the causes that have led to the crisis of the democracies as well as the people's republics will everywhere—except in England, which had its Kipling—encounter the superstructure of a state ideology whose modern ancestor was Hegel.

But where, as Hegel might have asked, is the world spirit riding today? Today, in the latter half of the sixties, we are at the beginning of a period of coexistence. Slowly and not without relapses, an attempt is being made to put an end to the postwar era of Cold War between two power blocs with precisely delimited spheres of interest and different forms of government. This change has not come about through reason and understanding alone. It has, in part, been necessitated by the atomic stalemate between the Soviet Union and the United States, yesterday's deadly enemies, which today are constrained by fear to join forces in defending their atomic monopoly against the claims of other states; and the People's Republic of China, the most recent vehicle of world revolution (and hence of the Hegelian world spirit), as well has also contributed to driving the Soviet Union, which (if we recall the claims it was raising only yesterday) seems almost to have become an advocate of gradual change, closer to the West.

At first sight, and against the background of the Cold War, we should like to welcome the new era of coexistence; but our very first glimpse of this power-plus-power alliance inclines us to skepticism: we discern signs suggesting that the East-West tension may turn into a North-South tension, because neither the South American nor the new African countries participate in the East-West détente; already they see themselves as the "Third World," the "Have-Nots," and demand to share in the wealth of the rich democracies and people's republics. Thus isolated, the Third World sees itself faced with the task of taking over the world revolution either in the train of China or according to the example of Castro; though their knowledge of Hegel comes to them at third or fourth hand, Hegel's world spirit is beginning to befuddle the countries of the Third World, to inspire them with faith in the absolute state. The manifestations of world-wide unrest, extending from the Cultural Revolution in China via the war in Vietnam and the Near Eastern conflict to the generalized, and in East and West equally impotent, youth protests against the established state apparatuses, are mutually complementary: in the East bloc countries, for example, sizable groups of intellectuals protest against the intervention, motivated by power politics and possibly anti-Semitism, of their governments in favor of the Arab nations, while the students in the Western democracies protest against the American political commitment in Vietnam and the subservience of their parliaments to corporate interests. Imperturbably as the government bureacracies of East and West try to carry on as usual, and succeed, the Cold War fronts have not only relaxed but have also become blurred. Moreover, in the Eastern as well as the Western power bloc, the obsolete Cold War institutions continue to operate, and whenever the always inadequate attempts at coexistence encounter obstacles or setbacks, these institutions resort to the Stalinist or anti-Communist vocabulary and find ready ears. But since the ideology of Stalinism and the ideology of anti-Communism, both of which draw their nourishment from Hegel's theory of the power state, must be held responsible for the long-concealed but now visible crises in the people's republics and parliamentary democracies, the idea of coexistence finds us unprepared or bogged down in the old rut. We are moving toward a coexistence not of peoples but only of atomic weapons systems restricted to the U.S.A. and the U.S.S.R.

The present book deals almost exclusively with the politics of the Federal Republic and the German Democratic Republic. It may be thought that in times of such universal confusion I should have devoted more attention to the world at large. It was by design that I limited my scope to Germany, and I stand by my design. For only if we are strong enough to resist the erosion of our constitutional government, only if we renounce Hegelian principles and fight our way through to a parliamentary democracy that is not subservient to pressure groups, shall we be strong enough to help the nations of the Third World without dragging them into a new dependency.

This volume consists of political speeches written and delivered from 1956 to 1967,[1] open letters to political figures, and an article in which I expressed my immediate reaction to the Great Coalition. The obituary of Konrad Adenauer was recorded for television but never broadcast. Of the three open letters, only one to Willy Brandt received an answer. My attempt as a citizen and a writer to write and speak about politics directly and as far as possible without the help of literary fiction, and my concomitant vote for the Social Democratic Party, have recently moved a few writers whom I had every reason to respect as political adversaries to abandon reasoned argument and vent their political hostility in

---

[1] The reference is to the German edition of Günter Grass's political writings, *Über das Selbstverständliche*, Neuwied and Berlin, 1968.

terms of innuendo and occasional slander. But I shall not dwell on this, because my subject is not the crisis among writers, which after all is merely a reflection of the more general crisis of democracy.

As we have said, the crisis is general. But it varies from country to country and from democracy to democracy. I will therefore distinguish between the crisis of certain democracies which can be limited, accelerated or halted on a regional basis, and the worldwide crisis of democracy, for which no regional remedy exists.

The world crisis dominates the regional crises especially because the democracies have endeavored, since the outbreak of the Cold War, to oppose the Communist world with a counter-ideology. I am referring to the pseudo-ideology of anti-Communism, which has been the main cause of the crisis of democracy. By seeing fit to treat Spain, Portugal and today the Greek military dictatorship as parts of the free world, by duplicating the Communist Iron Curtain with a democratic iron curtain, the democracies have cut themselves off from the possibility of social and political evolution; they have built up, as an ideological antithesis to Communism, a liberal (read: capitalist) freedom, intolerant of anything that smacks even remotely of Communism. Joseph McCarthy was not a purely American phenomenon; he had his imitators, and not only in West Germany. True, McCarthy has long been dead, but the self-corruption of a society which had made possible the subterfuge of anti-Communism, and all the many variants of McCarthyism, is still with us. The benefit of the democratic victory over fascist dictatorship was lost in the ideological struggle against Communism, when democracy and the democracies, lacking confidence in their own strength, isolated themselves, avoided contact with their political opponent, sniffed out the demonic enemy in every corner, and engaged in semifascist practices in the hope of defeating a Communism which for its part feared, and continues to fear, nothing so much as the unequivocal alternative of an evolutionary democracy.

For more than twenty years every attempt to free Western democracy from its reactionary strait jacket was defamed as open Communism or crypto-Communism. The anti-Communism enthroned in the West is the greatest triumph Communism could have achieved. It struck keen-sighted democrats blind. Like the "specter of Communism" in the Communist Manifesto, it haunted the world, fostering a political superstition which opened the door wide to the modern forms of witch hunt. This explains why parliamentary democracies have supported a corrupt feudal system in Persia, this is what made it possible for the anachronistic dictators of Spain and Portugal to stand side by side with Konrad Adenauer on the platform of anti-Communism; while today the United States and its sullen satellites support the dictator Ky merely because he calls himself an anti-Communist, just as the Soviet Union and its equally sullen satellites support the dictator Nasser merely because he represents himself as socialist, anticapitalist, anti-imperialist, etc. Ky and Nasser are the pictures on those doubly marked cards with which poker is played for power and influence all over the world. The terror of the Stalinist era, the crushing of the Hungarian uprising, the annexation of Tibet by Communist China are followed, on the same level, by the war in Vietnam. There in the extreme situation of war and here in our peaceful merry-go-round of proportionally distributed offices, the crisis of democracy is manifest: a corrupted Communism that has developed into a dictatorship of the bureaucracy is confronted by democracies whose parliaments are subservient to lobbies, whose formally free elections have more and more become a farce. A dubious coexistence will soon be possible; already every alternative is vanishing.

Times of general stagnation tend to foster demands for the radical transformation of all existing social systems. A new theory of revolution emanating from the West Coast of the United States is now making itself heard in Europe, especially at the universities in the ranks of the student protest movement. The proponents of this theory speak of a third revolution. Some naïvely taking their cue from Mao, others invoking the writings of the sociologist Herbert Marcuse, they aspire to do away both with bureaucratic Communism and with parliamentary democracy. Since in Europe there is no class that would have an interest in carrying out such a third revolution, Marcuse and his disciples put their hopes in the Third World, the "poor nations" which, as they see it, are locked in revolutionary conflict with the "possessor" nations, Communist as well as democratic.

It would be easy to laugh off this revolutionary thesis as a typical product of classroom revolutionaries. Nevertheless I should like to call attention to the fact that not only the justified student protests, but the present hare-brained or resolute attempts at revolution are direct and spontaneous evidence of the crisis of democracy. Because the protests give an impression of helplessness, because they demonstrate the political impotence of the young in our established society, because the debate is no longer between fathers and sons but between grandfathers and grandsons, the settled bourgeoisie can hardly feel threatened, especially since experience has shown that once the protesting youth marry and start worrying about their children and careers, they stop protesting. But the crisis of democracy might well continue and deepen until a *coup d'état* comes from the Right—and we all know what that looks like.

The health of German democracy has always been precarious. Yet, though often interrupted, its history is not without continuity. Several times over the last hundred years its achievements great and small, its justified or fulsome hopes, have been destroyed by frivolity or violence, only to be revived again. Imperfect and marked with every symptom of failure, democracy in Germany has at every rebirth presented the image of a torso. The German Federal Republic—according to its constitution a provisional entity, in practice a separate, exclusively West German state—lives, if only unconsciously, in this democratic tradition, fed on the one hand by archaeological industry and on the other hand permanently endangered by the speculation of Leftist as well as Rightist reactionaries, who look upon parliamentary democracy as the antechamber of dictatorship. The Federal Republic has been immune to temptations from outside; the semi-authoritarian French example has been taken up only in oratory. For all the harm it has done, even anti-Communism as a counter-ideology has not yet seriously endangered the foundations of the Federal Republic, but it has paved the way for the depreciation of the highest state offices: a former National Socialist as Chancellor has nullified all our efforts to become a creditable democracy; a man with an obscure past and erratic manners is President.[1] With the perseverance of a banal comic-strip figure who gives us an easy laugh week after week, he has degraded his high office to a point which I am inclined to call subversive. A further danger to parliamentary democracy in the Federal Republic is the notorious, increasing and increasingly courted concentration of newspapers and periodicals known as the Springer press. In Axel Cäsar Springer the Federal Republic has found a co-chancellor, who is accountable to no parliament, who cannot be voted out of office, who has set up a state within the state without alarming the guardians of our constitution. Hard as Herr von Thadden and the N.P.D. may be trying to destroy democracy from the Right by the old familiar methods; eager as the radical Left may be to take their Marcuse at his word at the risk of misunderstanding him—the House of Springer is a far greater danger than Rightist or Leftist impatience with democracy.

Quite apart from the scandalous espionage service of the House of Springer or the deplorable quality of its output, the sheer concentration of power represented by the Springer press makes it a threat to the survival of the Federal Republic as a democracy. Yet there is good reason to doubt that the Parliament

[1] The reference is to Herr Lübke.

still has independence enough to demand and enforce the dissolution of this trust, especially as the Christian Democratic Party is dependent on Springer for its survival and the Social Democratic Party has learned to fear Springer. The democratic-minded citizen will just have to watch his newspaper reading habits. I for my part have discovered that the *Frankfurter Rundschau* carries information undistorted by opinion and that the *Süddeutsche Zeitung* offers sound political information, an acceptable feature article and an amusing local section that is not without interest to the North German reader. After all, what do we know about Bavaria?

We often hear the Great Coalition decried as the sole cause of the crisis of democracy, as though the crisis would be over if the Great Coalition came to an end. In my opinion the Great Coalition is a mere consequence of an older crisis. Actually the political relation of forces in the Federal Republic and the present pseudo-peace between the political adversaries of yesterday are the consequences of the parliamentary elections of autumn 1965. The failure of the C.D.U./C.S.U. was then apparent; the S.P.D. went into the elections with fresh forces, offering a perfectly realistic if not revolutionary alternative; and yet, though a change of government was imperative, the voters did not provide the majority necessary to bring it about. Despite all the arguments which could then—and which can perhaps even now—be adduced in favor of the Great Coalition, it remains, even if the adjective "necessary" is appended, an evil, because West German democracy is too young to withstand the side effects of this dubiously motivated concentration of power and come through unscathed. There is no ground for hope that the voters have meanwhile attained a maturity that would enable them in 1969 to give the party with the best political record a clear-cut majority. It is rather to be feared that Chancellor Kiesinger's political style—a sure-fire propaganda technique that reveals his schooling—will again result in a so-called "ladies' choice." Disastrous as were the consequences for the Federal Republic of the legislature of 1957 to 1961 with its absolute C.D.U./C.S.U. majority, there is no guarantee that we shall not have another such legislature. The most those of us who are too skeptical to hope that the Social Democrats will at last carry off the electoral victory (which, everything considered, they deserve) can expect is a prolongation of the present relation of forces. But that means a continuation of the Great Coalition and hence also of the creeping crisis of democracy. For political maturity presupposes recognition of the crisis and its causes. Recognition of the crisis would in itself signify a democratic desire to overcome it. Of this there is no sign. True, there is widespread dissatisfaction; true, the numerous symptoms of disintegration offer an opportunity to grumble and crack jokes (often enough the last vestiges of moral courage find their sole expression in parlor games based on the solecisms of our present President), but this widespread dissatisfaction is powerless to change anything—it cannot renew our society. Though subservient to pressure groups and already headed for Portugal, democracy still regards itself as the alternative, though it is already, and not only in West Germany, on the road to dictatorship. Democracy is not seriously endangered by the National Democrats in Germany, by Goldwater in the United States or by any Communist conspiracy. The party oligarchies, the mania for political pragmatism, the anonymity of proportional representation, the lobbies that paralyze the Parliament, the cessation of effective parliamentary control over the executive and the view of the state as an absolute that has been current since Hegel—these are the factors that are eroding the substance of democracy. Our democracy is an edifice which, hardly erected, cries out for restoration. Because I am afraid of restorers, I am reluctant to give the alert; for no sooner had the first cracks appeared in the walls than demolition workers appeared from the Left and Right. But neither

Eugen Gerstenmaier's[1] authoritarian conceptions, nor the aggres
sive sing-out of the Springer press, nor Rudi Dutschke's warmed-
up soviets, nor Herbert Marcuse's eloquent disgust with democracy can relieve the crisis of democracy. Democracy does not lack
revolutionaries—some of them even come from the best families
—what it lacks is radical democrats. As long as legal evolutionary
methods of reviving parliamentary democracy are available, no
revolution is needed, particularly since the only alternatives
offered by even those proponents of the revolutionary solution
who can be taken seriously were born long ago, fathered, it has
been said, by Hegel.

In 1967, for the first time in the Federal Republic, high school
and university students came out with political demands. The self-
interested consensus of their fathers and grandfathers no longer
arouses mere sporadic protest; an opposition has arisen which
calls itself (or is called) extraparliamentary. Will it be persevering enough to seek and find its way to the Parliament? If this
opposition is to be taken seriously by its opponents as a political
force, it will have to overcome its Leftist-scholastic factional
struggles. Its task will be to understand the crisis of democracy on
the basis of its causes and to stem its course. Parliamentary democracy has not failed; what has happened rather is that the elective representatives of this highly differentiated and sensitive social form have let the power that was conferred upon them for a
limited time slip through their fingers.

I have made speeches, written letters and traveled all over the
country. My part was to speak, to make mistakes, to lose battles
and to start all over again. The aim of my efforts has been to
oppose skepticism, criticism and active political unrest to appeasements, promises of security and breaches of the constitution.
I have tried, and am still trying, to carry this active political unrest into the Social Democratic Party of Germany, in order that

---

[1] President of the Bundestag, member of the C.D.U.

criticism should not become an end in itself and contribute to the general paralysis, but should bring about changes.

On September 11th, Vice-Chancellor and Foreign Minister Willy Brandt, speaking on the television program "Panorama," said: "The parties have no monopoly in the expression of political opinion. In our state every individual citizen and consequently every group of citizens have a right to express themselves. This right must not be infringed upon."

It is up to us to take Willy Brandt at his word and to concentrate the political power of the extraparliamentary opposition, for in the autumn of 1969 the electorate of the Federal Republic will be called upon to vote.

To the question: "Where do you stand today?" I reply: "I remain a Social Democrat."

VIOLENCE REHABILITATED

On Holy Thursday, 1968, a youth named Bachmann, an
admirer of Hitler, shot and critically wounded Rudi
Dutschke, the leader of a militant Berlin student group. As
a result of this attempted murder, there were violent student
demonstrations during Easter week. The following
speech was delivered by Günter Grass on May 1, 1968, in
Hildesheim, and published in Der Spiegel, *May 1968.*

Ladies and gentlemen:

Only a few years ago the Federal Republic presented the image of a humdrum middle-class society, characterized by hard work, security, law and order, and political lethargy.

And now suddenly the Germans have been seized with unrest. The younger generation, only yesterday well behaved and fully adjusted to the existing order, are in a turmoil; they protest, demonstrate, and laugh at the rules of our domesticated democracy. Their fathers pat them on the back and tell them they don't realize how well off they are, but it doesn't go down, because the chasm between the theory and the practice of government is open for all to see, and none of the usual cloaks is big enough to cover it.

Even at the family board fathers are called to account: "Look here, Greece is a member of NATO and NATO is supposed to be defending freedom. Look here, when the Americans use napalm, it's a war crime, isn't it?"

And Father utters words of reassurance, sweats and utters more words of reassurance. He talks about power blocs and spheres of interest, and points out that the other side does the same thing. And he says he won't stand for Communist propaganda at the dinner table.

But it would be a grave mistake to suppose that the dissatisfaction of the younger generation finds its sole reflection on the Left. Young people are also to be met with far to the Right, in the gathering places of the old Party comrades. These young people are at once nonpolitical and political. Themselves full of contradictions, they move about like bulls in a china shop in a society that does not dare to resolve its own contradictions. The youth protest movement has brought the fragility of our insufficiently established democracy into evidence. In this it has been successful, but it is far from certain where this success will lead: either it will bring about long-overdue reforms, ranging from student representation to parliamentary reform and the replacement of the NATO treaty by an all-European peace including the Warsaw Pact countries, or else nothing will happen, and then the uncertainty that has now been laid bare will provide false prophets with promising markets and free advertising.

Already there is a confusion of language: students try to enlighten the workers and are occasionally threatened with blows because they speak a jargon that no worker can understand. The cleavage deepens. Trade unionists and Social Democrats, in Berlin and elsewhere, mobilize the workers against the students. A helpless Chancellor regrets that the emergency laws are not yet in force to help him keep order. But the students' reply to this stereotype appeal to order is the appeal of a North Vietnamese politician. Since irrational slogans change nothing but merely stir up the masses and arouse long-familiar aggressions, violence has been rehabilitated in the Federal Republic. For months the mass-circulation papers of the Springer trust have been clamoring for energetic measures, for active "self-help," yet after the attempt to murder Rudi Dutschke they made a show of righteous indignation. And after the attempt on Dutschke's life the actions of certain student organizations, especially the S.D.S.,[1] unleashed a movement of counter-violence.

The outcome—two deaths in Munich—raises the question of responsibility. What I hold up to those who share the responsibility—the spokesmen of the S.D.S. and of the Extraparliamentary Opposition—is that after the attempt on Rudi Dutschke's life they did nothing to prevent a spontaneous reaction in which indignation gave itself free rein and political considerations were left out of account. What the opponents of the student protest movement expected happened. Up to that point, it would have been possible to make broad sections of the public understand where the guilt lay; this emotional reaction inevitably effaced the beginnings of reflection. There ought to have been a preparatory pause, followed by well-organized demonstrations calculated to enlighten the public. Instead, there was an emotional reaction without political content. And now the question arises: Who was responsible?

But thus far this grave mistake has only provoked Scholastic discussions: Where does violence begin? Where does it stop? Violence against persons, no; violence against objects, yes; but when objects are used by persons, when the throwing of stones gets out of control, then Scholastic discussion must cease.

I have not come here to make a secret of my skepticism. May 1st is a political holiday, a summons to speak frankly. For the results of the elections in Baden-Württemberg cannot be glossed over. Even if Minister of Economics Karl Schiller has led the West German economy out of the pit, things will continue to go

---

[1] Socialist Student League.

downhill with this country as long as the Great Coalition under the former National Socialist Kurt Georg Kiesinger blocks every alternative and makes the N.P.D. a respectable party with smiling prospects for the future.

The S.P.D. should abandon this alliance before it is destroyed by the alliance. The mistaken decisions of Party Chairmen Willy Brandt and Herbert Wehner must be reversed in order that this country may again have a strong opposition capable of development. The Social Democrats should look for their allies not to the right of themselves, but among the young protesters, now helpless and left to their own resources. Not only our parliamentary democracy, but also the oldest democratic party of Germany, is in need of far-reaching reforms. How could it allow shallow intrigue and petty bureaucracy to alienate first the Socialist Student League and then the Social Democratic University League from the party? The S.D.S. would not have veered toward utopianism and radicalism had it not been expelled from the S.P.D. I wish that this breach between the Left-socialist, argumentative youth and the S.P.D. could be mended. I wish Rosa Luxemburg's plea for the freedom to disagree might find a hearing on both sides. But who in this country is still willing to listen to a plea for tolerance?

Of course it is laudable to go on talking the language of reason. Of course every day offers an opportunity to mediate with little success between adversaries congealed in their positions. Of course it is morally rewarding to play the heroic fireman in the midst of incendiaries, and anyone who wants to can sit for quite some time rather uncomfortably—I speak from experience—between two stools until, yes, until he falls to the floor; that is the role of the liberal, the useful idiot in the service of one or the other side, the Simple Simon who still believes that a socialist democracy can be built by evolutionary methods.

All this would be normal, it might be all right to go on in the same way—with a vacation now and then—if there had not meanwhile been three deaths, if it weren't for the visible and the invisible N.P.D., if there were no danger that three deaths might lead to many more deaths, and if there were not strong indications that the visible and the invisible N.P.D. might openly unite.

Let us look back: On June 2, 1967, in Berlin the student Benno Ohnesorg was shot by Police Officer Karl-Heinz Kurras. Was that shot really fired by Kurras alone? What had to happen before a policeman—even if he was trigger-happy—could draw his pistol, remove the safety catch, and fire the fatal shot? The Springer papers, especially *Bild,* had been calling for violence, for "self-help." Hard desk work was needed to arouse the aggressive instincts of our people. How can they be put to sleep again?

Let us look back: On Holy Thursday three shots rang out on the Kurfürstendamm in Berlin. We know the marksman's name,[1] we have seen the list of his previous convictions, we are familiar with his legend as it has been so touchingly cooked up by the press. He had, so says his mother, only one friend: his motorcycle. He painted little pictures and hung them in the parlor. One of these little pictures was published in the press. And just as he painted and exhibited his pictures in his room, he himself was painted and his picture exhibited to the public: An odd-ball. A lunatic with a police record. A house painter. A very special case. Hence an outcast unrelated to our basically healthy society. No concern of ours . . . No concern of ours . . .

No less a man than Chancellor Kiesinger sent a message of sympathy to Frau Dutschke and thereupon proceeded to defend the National Democrats against the accusation of complicity. The students pointed at the House of Springer. The actual murder weapon, they declared, was the open and veiled appeals to violence of the Springer press, especially its Berlin papers. Violence

[1] The reference is to Bachmann, the would-be murderer of Rudi Dutschke, who had portraits of Hitler, painted by himself, hanging in his room.

was answered with violence, windowpanes were smashed, fires set, stones hurled and records thrown into disorder. The lone odd-ball and would-be murderer swelled into a trigger-happy army: He, the solitary friend of his motorcycle, had merely carried out the plans which busy pens on many desks had been sketching for many months.

Seldom has an otherwise so torn society been so involuntarily yet harmoniously united in a task—the task of singling out one odd-ball, lunatic and house painter from perhaps a hundred thousand odd-balls, and impelling him to reach for his pistol. But didn't this solitary odd-ball say that the murder of Martin Luther King had inspired him to pick himself out a King and shoot him down? Since we are chronically innocent, mustn't someone else be guilty, in this case the Americans? Let's face it. American models, good and bad, find in us their epigones. And since epigones can seldom answer for their own acts, the House of Springer likens itself to the persecuted Jews and the spokesmen of the protest movement liken themselves to the oppressed Negroes. It's hard to find heroic models in a mediocre democracy sicklied o'er with compromise; so we borrow. The true victims of persecution are defenseless against the falsification and banalization of their calvary.

This once again so disastrous German revolution and the counter-revolution it inevitably provoked are characterized by false notes, theatrical gestures and presumption. It has often seemed to me that revolutionary committees and police chiefs dig up scenes from historical revolutions and model their behavior on Eisenstein's films and on early documentaries. Seldom have newspapers and illustrated magazines found more rewarding material; seldom have police officers had such frequent occasion to convert their training into action and to proclaim the freedom of the nightstick; seldom has an extreme Rightist party acquired votes so cheaply. The elections in Baden-Württemberg were said to have proved that on the one hand there is no basis for a revolution but that on the other hand there are few barriers left to halt a *coup* from the right.

The Federal Republic, as we all know, has many faults; they are obvious. Arrogant politicians corrupted by power are expertly engaged in eroding the substance of the constitutional state. Yet this country has not deserved to have the House of Springer share in its government, extending its pressure even to the Parliament, or to be driven by a few desperate revolutionaries—desperate because there is no basis for their revolution—into a civil war hysteria which, to close the circle, provides the Springer press with banner headlines and the N.P.D. with new voters.

It has become fashionable either to lump the whole younger generation together in a blanket condemnation, or else to applaud it blindly on the ground that "the young people are our future." Neither attitude is free from opportunism. The area between these camps of Rightist and Leftist opportunism is not a comfortable place to live in. But since I see no reason for succumbing to hysteria, I am quite willing to put up with the discomfort, though the libelous statements of both camps offer material for a paper skyscraper.

Let Herr Kiesinger believe that he is expressing the will of the German people when he invokes authority and emergency laws; let Herr Springer continue to feel that rising circulation figures prove him right; let the leaders of the S.D.S. go on defining violence as coldly and technically as if the deaths of the last few weeks had resulted from traffic accidents; let all three of these tendencies and their following work hand in hand to demolish the already ramshackle edifice of democracy in this country—I for my part refuse to let my judgment be clouded by all-or-nothing theses. The justified protest movement of the young people, which is not limited to students, must be saved from irrationalism if it is to become effective and if an entire generation is not once again to relapse into apolitical resignation merely because its utopian goals could not be attained.

Who benefits by old-fashioned class-struggle positions? In Berlin and Hamburg students tried to stop Springer trucks. In both cases the drivers stepped on the gas. The outcome: two students seriously injured in Berlin and one in Hamburg. Can there be any more glaring and more frightening proof that misunderstanding between workers and students can and does foment hostility between workers and students?

And let's not have any talk about fundamental political antagonisms. No, it requires no political genius to throw light on the antagonisms between workers and students. A student of behavior patterns who has thus far concentrated his attention on the greylag goose or the common carp would know what to make of them. . . .

Ladies and gentlemen, I have no other weapon than the word, my possibilities are limited. This platform is available to me for only a short time. Since May 1st is a political holiday, I should like to devote the few minutes still at my disposal to a plea against any further hardening of positions. Totalitarian demands are being raised on both sides. On one side: "Expropriate Springer"; on the other, "Suppress the S.D.S." If these extremes are to be reconciled in an evolutionary, democratic spirit, not only must the Parliament and Herr Springer but also the S.D.S. begin to show some understanding. This organization is not monolithic; it comprises several groups which freely discuss their possibilities and manias together. Even if the remote political goals of the S.D.S. are not my goals, I recognize its achievement, especially as a promoter of university reform, but also as the motive force within the student protest movement. In both senses of the word, it *deserves* criticism, and it is up to us to provide that criticism.

My suggestion is that the S.D.S., especially in Munich and Berlin, where it has been at fault for fomenting irresponsible actions, should withdraw from its position of leadership, which is in any case questionable. I advise the S.D.S. to demand the resignation of the leaders of its Munich and Berlin groups. When after the events of June 2, 1967,[1] Mayor Albertz of Berlin, Senator Büsch and Police Chief Duensing were asked—and rightly so—to resign, they did indeed resign. Similarly the S.D.S. must acknowledge its mistakes and take the consequences, unless it wants to be more incorrigibly arrogant than the establishment it attacks.

At the same time I call on the Social Democratic University League to abandon its policy of solidarity at any price with its political allies, in other words, to stop covering the mistakes of the S.D.S. The student protest movement ceases to be convincing when it adopts the impure methods of its political adversaries.

But anyone who imagines that the only way to save democracy is to suppress the S.D.S. should consider the incalculable harm done to democracy by the mere fact that a former National Socialist has become Chancellor. There is no point in getting excited about the rapid growth of the N.P.D. as long as Herr Kiesinger, through the revalorization of his political past, revalorizes the N.P.D. Instead of suppressing the S.D.S., we should do better to ask ourselves whether our democratic form of government can stand up against such wanton devaluation of the office of Chancellor.

Yesterday in the course of a debate in the Parliament, Chancellor Kiesinger tried to explain the electoral success of the N.P.D. in Baden-Württemberg. He reeled off all manner of true and half-true explanations: the peasants' resentment of the government; the repercussions of the Easter disorders, and so on. And he tried to allay the alarm of our neighbors by defending the N.P.D.

---

[1] On this date, the state visit of the Shah of Iran in Berlin occasioned tumultuous student demonstrations during which the German student Ohnesorg was shot by Police Officer Kurras.

against the imputation that it was a new edition of National Socialism, a neo-Nazi party.

With his own special brand of eloquence he reduced the whole matter to the dimensions of a trifling misdemeanor which had been misinterpreted and overestimated by our neighbors. And not a word—in this he proved himself a master of the art of omission —about the part he himself had played, if only involuntarily, in helping this rising party to respectability.

In joining the Great Coalition the S.P.D. acquiesced in Herr Kiesinger's Chancellorship. The Social Democratic Party of Germany will bear the responsibility for this mistake for a long time to come. Two days before the conclusion of the Great Coalition I wrote Herr Kiesinger an open letter calling his attention to the consequences of his disastrous decision: "How are the young people of our country to find arguments against that party which died two decades ago but is being resurrected today as the N.P.D., if you burden the Chancellorship with the still very considerable weight of your past?"

If we wish to counter the N.P.D. with something more than the usual verbal appeasements, the parties represented in the Parliament, and first of all the S.P.D., must make up their minds to perform a political act. It is not yet too late to reverse the decision of January 1966. The Federal Republic offers any number of important political jobs that Kurt Georg Kiesinger could fill. But as a member of the National Socialist Party from 1933 to 1945 he should not permit himself, and we should not permit him, to hold the office of Chancellor.

So far, ladies and gentlemen, I have been obliged to concern myself almost exclusively with the extremist camps in this partly political, partly biological conflict. I should much rather speak of the authentic youth protest, which is aimed at reforms and evolutionary changes but finds less and less of a hearing. This is a job for the unions. They can promote discussion between workers and students and so counter the uncompromising extremism that threatens to create a ruinous division among our people. In particular the trade union press, which for years has been serving up tailor-made boredom, should open its ears to new ideas and its columns to the opinions of the young people, however contradictory and disturbing. . . . The young people are no longer willing to assume the debts of their fathers and grandfathers without discussion. The answer to their justified protest is not appeasement but reform.

A CHANCELLOR
WITH A PAST

Speech delivered May 9, 1968, at Technische Universität, Berlin.

Ladies and gentlemen:

It has become fashionable to believe that under the capitalist system democracy necessarily leads to fascism. This theory is as convenient as it is false. It is easy enough to show that the fascist threat to the parliamentary democracies of such capitalist countries as Holland, Switzerland, England and Scandinavia is minimal or nonexistent.

Conversely, what made Germany and Italy capitulate so quickly to National Socialism and fascism was the absence of a parliamentary, democratic tradition. In both cases, not only the system of free capitalist enterprise collapsed, but also the mutually hostile Communist and socialist organizations. The resistance of small liberal groups and of the Social Democrats had previously been broken by the simultaneous assault of the Communists and of the National Socialists or fascists.

The early history of Italian fascism is illuminating. Mussolini started out as a Left-wing socialist; while agitating in Switzerland, he became acquainted with anarchism; it was from an amalgam of socialism and anarchism that he found his way to fascism.

I maintain that the combination of socialism and anarchism can still lead to fascism. Moreover, it cannot be overlooked that the systems based on fascist and Stalinist ideologies have borrowed heavily from each other. In East Germany, for example, the whole style of the Free German Youth Organization and the People's Army shows the disastrous imprint of the direct transition from National Socialism to Stalinism.

In the German Democratic Republic it was possible to integrate the heritage of the Third Reich with Stalinism. In the Federal Republic, where no such possibility offered itself, the aftereffects of National Socialism have of late been manifested more openly and actively than ever.

I am referring not "only" to the extreme Rightist party of Herr von Thadden, with its National Socialism refurbished to look respectable, but also to a man who, having been a National Socialist from 1933 to 1945, is now Chancellor and as such is making National Socialism respectable, even if this is not his intention.

The National Democratic Party does not differ fundamentally from the National Socialist Party; it is "merely" a cruder version, just as National Socialism was a cruder version of Italian fascism. Its crudeness does not make the N.P.D. any less dangerous. For this party, as its proclamations and the election returns show, is merely the visible tip of an iceberg—of a compact mass beneath the surface—which has existed since the inception of the Federal Republic. As long as Konrad Adenauer—working in the spirit of a not yet founded N.P.D.—was able to gather those who were amenable to National Socialist ideas into the Christian Democratic Union, and as long as the Social Democrats as an opposition party were able to attract the protest vote that now goes to the National Democrats, the iceberg did not show its tip; and when it dared to do so, an occidental or Christian cloak was quickly thrown over it. One might in a pinch regard this integration of latently Nazi sections of the electorate as an achievement of Konrad Adenauer, but then we should have to say that this accomplishment, like so many of Adenauer's accomplishments, was nullified even before his death.

For as the Adenauer era drew to a close, the latent Nazi among the electorate were set free, and once Adenauer had stepped down, his successor, Ludwig Erhard, with the support of President Gerstenmeier and of certain mass-circulation newspapers, encouraged the resurgence of nationalism. In its beginnings, however, the National Democratic Party was hampered by the widespread feeling that as the successor of the National Socialist Party it was somehow disreputable.

It was only when Kurt Georg Kiesinger, supported by the votes of the C.D.U./C.S.U. and the S.P.D., became Chancellor, when the disastrous revalorization of his political past led to a revalorization of the Nazi origins of the N.P.D., that this barrier was removed; for if a former Nazi can become Chancellor, not only the petty hanger-on of former times but also a youngster for whom the Third Reich is ancient history can vote National Democrat with a clear conscience.

We have seen how, after the elections in Baden-Württemberg, Chancellor Kurt Georg Kiesinger attempted in a speech to the Parliament to explain the N.P.D. to an alarmed world. Certain passages in this speech sound as if the Chancellor had been trying to present his own past in a more reassuring light. Recently he has announced his intention of publishing a set of documents presumably intended to prove that he personally never killed anybody, but only sat harmlessly at his desk. Right now they are looking for a historian to give this collection of documents a scientific aura. No one doubts that a suitable historian will be found.

Kiesinger is taking his precautions. He wishes to anticipate the arrival of documents from the East German Republic. But why wait? I myself have at my disposal some four pounds of documents bearing witness to the intricacy and tedium of National Socialist bureaucratic routine. The Propaganda Ministry under Goebbels and the Ministry of Foreign Affairs under Ribbentrop both claimed jurisdiction in certain matters. Herr Kiesinger, who as deputy section head in the Ministry of Foreign Affairs served as an intermediary between the two ministries, may see fit to interpret the resultant disputes as a variety of inner emigration, or even as an indication of resistance. But make no mistake: Wherever the foreign propaganda of Ribbentrop and Kiesinger was at work—in France, Yugoslavia, the Netherlands, the Soviet Union, etc.—the quiet humdrum labors of a hard-working National Socialist brought death, all the more so as the propaganda machines both of Goebbels and of Ribbentrop pursued the common aim of cloaking the war crimes of National Socialism beneath high-sounding words.

Even if Herr Kiesinger assures us that he is no longer a National Socialist—and why should he be?—his tone remains that of a man who is trying to reassure people and to make the offensive seem inoffensive. Today he no longer employs his eloquence to cover the crimes of the National Socialists; he seeks instead to submerge the National Socialist inheritance of the N.P.D. and his own National Socialist past beneath a river of words.

Because of this alliance between Kurt Georg Kiesinger and the N.P.D., even if it is involuntary, it will not be possible to combat the N.P.D. effectively until Kurt Georg Kiesinger ceases to burden the office of Chancellor with the weight of his past.

I own that it will be a hard fight. In its attempt to point up the discrepancy between the theory and the practice of government in the Federal Republic, the youth protest movement has thus far turned its attention neither to the Kiesinger phenomenon nor to the interaction between the N.P.D. and Kiesinger.

When Kurt Georg Kiesinger became Chancellor, only a few spoke up against this devaluation of the office of Chancellor. Nor did our neighbors, though rightly alarmed by the growth of the N.P.D., show any unwillingness to put up with Kiesinger. Perhaps the public failed to protest against Kiesinger's Chancellorship because they were used to seeing Nazis in high government office. But this will not deter me from continuing to cry out against the devaluation of the office of Chancellor by Kurt Georg Kiesinger.

The day before he became Chancellor I wrote an open letter to Kurt Georg Kiesinger, then Premier of Baden-Württemberg. I called his attention to the consequences that his Chancellorship would have for the Federal Republic. I received no answer.

Since then I have several times, here in Berlin and in various cities of the Federal Republic, pointed out that the Chancellorship of Kurt Georg Kiesinger would involve the Federal Republic, both at home and in its relations with foreign countries, in consequences for which not Herr Kiesinger but a generation which knows the Nazi period only from hearsay will have to pay. Except for the usual threatening letters there has been no response.

At the S.P.D. party congress in Nuremberg and on the "Speaking Frankly" program of the South German Radio in Stuttgart, I repeated what cannot be repeated often enough. Among the many expressions of disagreement elicited by my remarks, one was an open letter from Dean Heinrich Grüber of Berlin.

Dean Grüber writes:

"As one of the few men now alive who, with full consciousness of his responsibility, not only lived through the period which began more than thirty-five years ago but also suffered for his opinions, I feel justified in saying that in my opinion no one who did not himself withstand the acid test to which many were then subjected should presume to pass judgment on the conduct of men at that time."

Dean Grüber is a man of the Resistance, and if he denies me the right to speak of the National Socialist period and its consequences down to our own day, I am obliged to answer more plainly than I might have wished.

I take the liberty of reading you my open letter of reply.

Berlin, May 8, 1968

My dear Dean Grüber,

In your open letter to me you maintain that no one who did not consciously experience the Nazi period and—as you say—withstand the "acid test" is entitled to pass judgment on the conduct of men at that time. Your categoric decree is calculated to prevent me from continuing to point out how irresponsible it was to make Kurt Georg Kiesinger, a Nazi from 1933 to 1945, Chancellor.

I shall not observe your order to keep silent because to keep silent about Kiesinger would mean to keep silent about the new edition of the National Socialist Party, the National Democrats.

If the Nazi past of Gutmann, President of the Baden-Württemberg section of the N.P.D., is regarded as an argument against him, there can be no reason to plead extenuating circumstances for Kurt Georg Kiesinger. Even a boy of twenty has every right to come to this conclusion. I fail to see how you as a Christian can contest the right of the new generation to join in the discussion and to pass judgment. If only those who were there in person were entitled to speak, it would be difficult for you to invoke the Apostle Paul, who belonged to a later generation and did not personally participate in the life of Christ, yet delivered himself of resounding judgments concerning it, which carry weight to this day.

However, to meet your requirements: I was there in person. Born in 1927, I had the opportunity, thanks to the solicitude of Herr Kiesinger's generation, to become an Air Force auxiliary at the age of fifteen, a soldier at sixteen and a prisoner of war at seventeen. Because Herr Kiesinger and his generation wished to spare us nothing, literally nothing, I was also privileged to make the acquaintance of fear and to look on as half of a company of sixteen-year-olds were killed or wounded in their very first battle. Of course Herr Kiesinger had no way of knowing that such things would happen. To the very end he was busy as deputy section head, co-ordinating the foreign propaganda of the Ministry of Foreign Affairs under Ribbentrop with the propaganda of the Propaganda Ministry under Goebbels. That must have been a hard job. In matters of propaganda the two ministries were in competition, their jurisdictions overlapped and disputes were frequent. Herr Kiesinger was often called upon to mediate between them. But I am certain that there will be any number of reputation-menders who will try to persuade the public that this activity as a go-between amounted to resistance against the Nazi regime.

To put it plainly: Herr Kiesinger was a small, insignificant Nazi, who went along because everybody else went along. In 1933 Herr Kiesinger was not an adolescent hothead but a grown man. He should have known whom he was serving with his intellectual capacities.

I have before me the twelve guidelines for active German propaganda in foreign countries, issued in 1941. As the document shows, Herr Kiesinger was cognizant of these guidelines: he was under obligation to adhere to them, and, as his trip to occupied France demonstrates, he also translated them into political reality.

Guideline 1: "Germany is winning the war." Guideline 5: "The Jew Roosevelt is striving for Jewish world domination." Guideline 8 informed Herr Kiesinger that "Bolshevism is the greatest danger to mankind. Hitler has freed the world of this danger." Immediately thereafter Kiesinger, the Catholic, could read: "The Archbishop of Canterbury is praying for the anti-Christians." Under No. 10, Herr Kiesinger read: "Germany is fighting for social justice against Jewish-plutocratic exploitation."

I can imagine that on reading No. 12—"Hitler's victory will mean a thousand years of prosperity, happiness and peace"—Herr Kiesinger may have reacted with a certain Swabian skepticism.

But even assuming that he had occasional doubts, his imperfect faith in final victory did not prevent him on October 28, 1941, from sending out the following directive:

"As already communicated by telephone, the following telegram has been received from the embassy in Buenos Aires:

" 'Reports of bad treatment of foreign workers employed in Germany being broadcast by news services B.B.C. London and relayed by local Prieto and Splendid stations. To correct these false reports suggest reportage with foreign workers at the microphone to be broadcast by German short-wave stations. . . .'

"Request acceptance suggestion."

My dear Dean Grüber, I am not going to torture you with items from the records of a period that you experienced as a man of the Resistance.

I am horrified that we should still be obliged to stir up these bitter dregs—and, to make matters worse, that we are obliged to do so before the East German government publishes its heralded documents on Chancellor Kiesinger's past. But no one can relieve us of the need to make a decision. Either we show our respect for the men of the Resistance, the murdered millions, the German soldiers who were sent to their deaths by a criminal system, or we make a mockery of them by setting down Herr Kiesinger's political opportunism as respectable realism.

If you as a man of the Church, which is ordinarily only too prone to moral judgment, should now, when the authority of the state is in question, leave morality to the Hymnal, your Church will be obliged to consider appending the new commandment, "Act opportunistically," as a footnote to the Ten Commandments. But even if we wished to ignore moral misgivings as "merely moral," the political consequences of the blunder of December 1966 ought at least to carry some weight.

This country is having a hard time regaining the confidence of its neighbors in the East and West. War crimes committed by the Germans and from the very start glossed over and misrepresented by the German propaganda machine in which Herr Kiesinger played a part, war crimes without their parallel in history have left a more painful memory in the affected countries—the Soviet Union, France, Holland, etc.—than in Germany, the home of those who still bear or share the responsibility.

The political past of Chancellor Kurt Georg Kiesinger is a millstone around the neck of German foreign policy. How can we expect to diminish our neighbors' distrust is we permit, and continue to permit, a former National Socialist to be Chancellor? The rehabilitation of his National Socialist past raises the standing of the N.P.D. and at the same time undermines the meager credit which the Federal Republic has built up in the East and West at the cost of painstaking effort.

Yours
Günter Grass

CZECHOSLOVAKIA 1968

Address delivered on September 8th in Basel, Switzerland.
Published in Die Zeit, October 4, 1968.

Ladies and gentlemen:

This is not a protest meeting. Protest is a reaction to the injustice of the day. The injustice remains and the protest dies down. Everyday life starts in again. Czechoslovakia crowded Vietnam out of the news, and now Biafra is taking the place of Czechoslovakia. Meanwhile the papers report earthquakes, presidential elections, more protest meetings, and fluctuations of the stock market.

So it might be a good idea to suspend our reactions to the headlines, which as often as not spring from a mere sense of obligation, to look back—because the occupation of Czechoslovakia is already behind us—and ask a few questions about our own attitude.

The questions are: Why is democratic socialism a matter of importance to us?

And: To what extent do we share the responsibility for the failure of democratic socialism?

It would be easy to prove that the applause of once uncompromising Cold Warriors, which rose to a clamor and then turned to telegenic lamentations when Czechoslovakia was occupied, was in part responsible for the Czechoslovakian tragedy.

But this is not the right place or the right audience for a speech about the last Cold War or the next. I am more concerned with the missed opportunities of the European Left, or at least that part of it which regards itself as radical or revolutionary.

For more than a year, ever since the writers Vaculik, Klima, Havel, Kundera, Kohout and Liehm made their accusing speeches against the neo-Stalinist regime of Antonin Novotny, then still in power, and began drafting plans for the future, the revolutionary Western European Left and the growing student protest movement have had ample opportunity to appreciate the daring efforts of the Czechs and Slovaks and to identify themselves with their cause.

But the students of Berlin and Paris did not take Vaculik or Havel as their model; their choice was photogenic and aesthetic: Che Guevara, the Argentine professional revolutionary, was enlarged to pin-up size. In other words: While the Czechoslovakian reformers were trying to put through their reform under the most discouraging conditions and to overcome obstacles which, as we have recently seen, are still insuperable, the Western radical Left —also termed the New Left—indulged in romantic revolutionary gestures. Without a program, expressing itself in a jargon that no one could understand, this Left succeeded in dissipating the protest movement and in provoking the radical Right. The fears aroused by the election returns in Baden-Württemberg were soon fully borne out in France: never has reactionary sentiment been stronger in Western Europe than in the summer of this year.

How could the Stalinist reactionaries in the Soviet Union have been expected to sit still when their conservative brothers in Western Europe were so unmistakably successful? They attacked. The police state mentalities of the East and West have developed a negative but harmonious coexistence that is well illustrated by the police actions in Berlin and Paris and the action of the occupying powers in Czechoslovakia.

But though the brutality of international power politics is the same everywhere, the Western New Left saw little or no reason to take notice of the New Left in Czechoslovakia, let alone support it. It pursued different and often contrary aims.

While the Czechs and Slovaks were demanding the liberalization of their system and the toleration of disagreement, here in our country tolerance was rejected and liberalism denounced as the mortal enemy of revolution.

While in Prague and Bratislava the theory of reform had immediately to be tested in practice, here reform was slandered as reformism and theory carried to the point of hair-splitting. Once again, our revolutionaries wanted all or nothing. And the result was: nothing.

While the Czechoslovakian students, writers and scientists were working in a calm, businesslike way, the Western European Left was indulging in revolutionary dramatics. The New Left in Czechoslovakia has temporarily succumbed to the superior power of reaction; the Western New Left has failed through its own fault and through its inability to understand the lesson of Prague. Its thinking bears a share in the responsibility. Today its former spokesmen are trying, in resignation, to blend with the landscape; nevertheless this indictment will find them.

What I have said about the responsibility of the intellectuals of the radical Left does not refer primarily to the minority of radical students, most of them scions of upper-middle-class families, who expanded their protest against their parents into a protest against the Establishment as such; I am referring chiefly to the intellectuals of my own generation, who irresponsibly neglected to give the students the criticism they needed and did their best to participate in the blind activism of a pseudo-revolutionary movement.

For a whole year I tried, in a series of speeches running parallel to my open correspondence with Pavel Kohout, to draw the attention of students, and of the writers of my generation, to the reform of socialism in Czechoslovakia. With little success. I shall not forget the laughter of the gilded young revolutionaries and the indifference of the revolutionary elite. Nor the arrogance: "Those people lack revolutionary perspective. Why, what this Professor Sik is aiming at is pure liberalism or, still worse, social democracy."

Delegations of the Socialist Student League went to Prague and with Teutonic presumption tried to teach the Czechs and Slovaks a little academic Marxism. The polite but secretly disappointed reaction of the Czechoslovakian students to the West German visitors is summed up in the words of a young historian from Charles University in Prague: "They don't know anything, but they know it all." An example: In a collection of articles on "Students and Power," the writer Hans Magnus Enzensberger expresses the following judgment on the Prague student movement: "The documents bear witness to an extremely limited horizon. Their political substance is meager. . . . The German Democratic Republic is regarded as a foreign enemy. If they have any sympathies in their own camp, it is for Rumania and Yugoslavia. The Cuban and Chinese conceptions and experiences are ignored or rejected *en bloc*."

Measured against the demands of Hans Magnus Enzensberger, the Prague attempt at reform was held to be meager and unattractive. In other words, Alexander Dubcek's cautiously formulated program for a democratic socialism could make no headway against the cult of Che Guevara. All mention of a serious, carefully thought-out movement—even then impeded by unavoidable compromises and today interrupted by power politics—was drowned out by rhythmic stamping and in lieu of arguments by loud cries of "Ho Chi Minh!"

Anyone who has ever attempted to gain a hearing for the Czechoslovakian attempt at reform knows what brilliant disciples the Josef Goebbels of other days has found among the West European Left-wing radicals of today.

Will the occupation of Czechoslovakia have a sobering effect on the revolutionaries in the exquisite salons of Rome, in the Berlin Republican Club and in the Paris Latin Quarter? I see no reason whatsoever to embellish the disaster of the West European Left with fronds of hope. This community, verbally so radical, has always sought and found an escape: yesterday it was Cuba; now that Fidel Castro has approved the occupation of Czechoslovakia, Mao remains available free of charge. And should this last refuge become untenable, there is always the looking glass: Narcissus always manages to survive. But now that false solidarities have been exposed, perhaps our students will realize what charlatanism they fell for when they saw the future in an obsolete Soviet system, while only a few miles away, in Prague and Bratislava, a first attempt was being made to overcome the bipartite division of the world and to bridge the gulf between Communism and Social Democracy.

If today we ask ourselves whether we can help Czechoslovakia, we should, I believe, dispense with gratuitous gestures of sympathy, and take up the challenge of democratic socialism.

To me as a Social Democrat this means that in the same measure as Communism in Czechoslovakia has been striving for a *rapprochement* with its fellow products of European enlightenment, namely, the fundamental democratic rights, Social Democracy should try to break with its short-sighted concentration on immediate economic ends and work toward a modern socialism in which all who are qualified to do so participate in decisions and responsibilities and so exert a democratic control over the organs of power and the instruments of production. Marx is not an infal-

lible Church Father. The dogmatic exegesis of his works has led
to disastrous economic blunders in the people's republics. Today
we know that when basic industry was expropriated in the people's republics it did not become the property of the people but
was handed over to a new owner—the state. But state capitalism
is not an alternative to private capitalism. In all the people's republics state-controlled unions made it impossible from the outset
for the workers to participate in industrial management. We
ought to be just a little proud of the fact that in the parliamentary
democracies the unions have managed to maintain their independence of the state. Let them make use of their independence
and answer the call from Prague and Bratislava. If the Czechs
and Slovaks with their reform have met the Western socialist
parties halfway, the question arises: Do we want to stay in our old
rut, or are we too prepared to go halfway?

Recently Willy Brandt, the West German Minister of Foreign
Affairs, made a speech in Geneva. He pointed out that it is no
longer a question of petty security, of short-term interests and
comfortably rising prosperity; his demand for world-wide renun-
ciation of the use of force and his condemnation of all military
intervention were uttered at a time when the casualty figures in
the various theaters of war are mounting faster than the gross
national product. The genocide in Biafra, for which all—and I
mean all—social systems bear their share of responsibility, is the
most terrifying consequence of East-West power politics: English
and Soviet, Swiss and Czechoslovakian, Portuguese and French
arms are competing on African soil—an inhuman expression of
what might still cynically be called "aid to underdeveloped countries."

Now that Czechoslovakian socialism, despite its temporary re-
pression, has become a world-wide necessity, it is to be hoped that
it will see its first task in the co-ordination of Eastern and Western aid to underdeveloped countries. First of all, it is incumbent
on the Socialist and Social Democratic parties of Western Europe

to give content to the thus far empty concept of coexistence by putting forward a program for co-ordinated aid that will put an end to the power-political competition between East and West.

Two overfed world powers have converted stupidity into armored divisions and atomic warheads. And we sit in between, permanently threatened by the good-natured pats on the back of one or the other giant. At last we have understood the lesson of Prague.